Architectural and
Building Design

Architectural and Building Design:
An Introduction

Michael Young
Dip Arch, MSc, RIBA, FRAIA

Heinemann: London

William Heinemann Ltd
10 Upper Grosvenor Street, London W1X 9PA

LONDON MELBOURNE TORONTO
JOHANNESBURG AUCKLAND

© Michael Young 1986
First published 1986

British Library in Cataloguing in Publication Data
Young, Michael
  Architectural and building design: an introduction
  1. Architecture
  I. Title
  721   NA2510

ISBN 0 434 92448 2

Photoset in Great Britain by
Rowland Phototypesetting Ltd, Bury St Edmunds, Suffolk
and printed by St Edmundsbury Press
Bury St Edmunds, Suffolk

Contents

Preface

Many books on the theory of design, (both architectural and other), have been written, but invariably these have been geared to the architect or designer and not to other members of the production team.

The aim of this book is to lead the non-designer to the philosophies and processes involved in the design of buildings; to introduce architectural design to those members of the design team, especially quantity surveyors, building surveyors, estate managers, planners, construction managers, structural engineers, service engineers, and landscape architects together with architectural and other technicians all of whom will have a knowledge of building technology and many of whom will be versed in building economics.

This book is planned to cover the evolution of design; the design process; the constraints that affect design decisions including climate, site, technological, economic, and legal, together with the planning of buildings as well as aesthetics—which is seen as having to reflect the logical answer to the problems posed by the planning and constraints. The reaction of the user and special problems such as designing for disabled persons and building conservation are also discussed.

In the design of buildings technology cannot be ignored, nor can economics, but these are consciously played down here because this book is seen as complementing the many books on construction, services, and building economics that are available.

This book is not intended to be a handbook on 'how to do it' and thus does not contain technical information on design requirements (toilet space, etc.) but references are given which, in many cases, do provide these.

Acknowledgements

As any author knows, the production of a book of this nature cannot be done without the co-operation of many people and this volume is no exception.

First of all, I would like to thank the many colleagues who offered advice and help at The Polytechnic of the South Bank, not only my academic friends but also the library, secretarial and technical staff as well as the students who contributed in their own specialist way. I would, however, like to single out two colleagues who devoted a considerable amount of their precious time to reading and advising on my drafts, namely Dr Alan Morris and Bridget Jackson. Their carefully considered and critical comments were most valuable, nevertheless any errors or omissions in the book must remain my sole responsibility.

I would also like to thank Lesley Woodland for typing the draft for me whilst at home awaiting the birth of her first daughter, Alice and to Alan Halls for his help on photographic expeditions and on the jacket design.

Much effort was expended by a number of people to enable me to obtain all the photographs that I needed and here I would particularly like to thank Julian Feary and my two long-standing friends from student days in Australia, Bruce Lincoln and Frank Clarke.

Finally my thanks to the publishers for their help, advice, and hard work.

Plates

Figures

Introduction

The use of the words 'building' and 'architectural' in the title of this book occur because of the confusion that exists in many people's minds over the demarkation between buildings and works of architecture. All works of architecture are, or were, buildings but the converse is not true.

Probably the simplest demarkation is that works of architecture are consciously designed whereas buildings are just built. But this is an oversimplification. Architecture being an art, the mother of all arts, must infuse delight in the beholder and it is in this delight that we can see the difference between buildings and works of architecture. This is not only the vital visual delight, both external and internal, but delight at using the 'building' in every respect—the ease of circulation, the acoustics, the spatial organisation, the blending of the building to its surroundings whether natural or man-made, and the climatic modifier for it must never be too hot, too cold, too humid, too dry, too draughty, too glary, or too dull. All of these factors combine to give true delight in a work of architecture.

Few buildings give delight in every respect but, providing the balance tilts massively in favour of delight, then the building will probably be accorded the title 'a work of architecture'. St Paul's Cathedral, London, is bad acoustically, the patrons of the Sydney Opera House get wet entering the building during rain, many of Frank Lloyd Wrights' buildings had inherent faults such as leaking roofs but all of these through conscious design and their ability to give great delight are considered to be architecture.

The difference between a building and a work of architecture has nothing to do with its size or with the fame of the design team. However, this distinction of conscious design remains uppermost in most people's minds until one thinks, perhaps, of a medieval barn which never saw any conscious design but gives true delight. Is it a building or a work of architecture? Then again what of some consciously designed office blocks or multi-storey blocks of flats—are they works of architecture or mere buildings?

In most cases, however, what we refer to as works of architecture will only have been achieved by very conscious design on the part of the whole design team, which for a medieval cathedral would comprise clergy, master mason and carpenter, workmen and artists and which nowadays includes not only the architect but also the structural and environmental engineer, the quantity surveyor, the estates surveyor, the landscape architect, the interior designer, the contractor, the client and, increasingly, the user.

I

The evolution of building design

Introduction

Present day observers of proposed and recently completed buildings will notice that buildings are now being built in a variety of styles, which differs not only from country to country but even within one country or even one town or city. This has not always been the case. In order to understand the present position it is necessary to have an appreciation of the evolution of building design.

Classical times

Building in the Western world commenced about 8,000 years ago along the Nile Valley and throughout the whole of the period of the Egyptian Empire remained a slow evolutionary process. Nevertheless, a clearly identifiable style emerged over the 5,000 years during which the empire flourished. The same is true of the work of the classical Greek period, when a very definite and superb architectural style developed in an evolutionary way. Later, the Romans took the classical Greek style and adapted it to their materials, techniques and slightly more vulgar taste. During the period of the Roman Empire the writer Vitruvius produced his work entitled *The Ten Books on Architecture* setting out very definite rules on many aspects of building and town design; many principles cited in these writings still apply to the present day and translations of the books are still available. Vitruvius's writings constitute the first recorded attempt to produce a set of guidelines or principles upon which building design could be based.

Medieval

After the fall of the Roman Empire most of Europe settled back into its pre-Roman way of life and throughout the Dark Ages building once more developed along evolutionary and local lines. As Europe emerged from these insular centuries a clearly identifiable style started to develop for the more important buildings such as churches and the monastic buildings, although its roots were essentially in the local vernacular traditions. Travel and conquest meant that a more universal style gradually became apparent although local traditions persisted and from about 1050 it became possible to distinguish between the styles of neighbouring countries. Throughout the Middle Ages this style, known as Gothic, evolved separately in each country although there is more that unites the architecture of Gothic buildings of different European countries than separates it.

The invention of the printing press by Gutenburg in 1454 made it possible to reproduce the written word much more economically than had hitherto been possible, but it was not until the seventeenth century that the first book on architectural principles was published; this was Andrea Palladio's *Quattro Libri dell' Architectura*, which was translated into English and published in Britain in 1715. Andrea Palladio was, nevertheless, instrumental in effecting the first real change in the appearance of British building.

Renaissance

The Renaissance started in Italy in the latter years of the fifteenth century and, aided by the printing press, gradually moved across Europe. As Britain became more and more prosperous, especially during the latter part of the sixteenth century, workmen were brought over from the Continent to carry out work on the more important houses and other buildings. They brought with them new ideas and executed their work using Renaissance details popular in their own countries.

This was the position when Inigo Jones visited Italy in the late sixteenth and early seventeenth centuries. In fact, it was during one of his stays there that he worked for Andrea Palladio and was impressed with his mentor's work. On his return to Britain he put the knowledge gained on his trip into effect with the design for a new palace in Whitehall, London and in the design for the Queen's house in Greenwich. Work stopped on the Queen's house before it was completed and only the Banqueting Hall of the palace was built, but by 1619 London had—in the Banqueting Hall—its first building built completely in this new Renaissance style, following the principles of Renaissance design as conceived by a pupil of Palladio.

Christopher Wren adopted and adapted this new style for.his

buildings. His first commission, the Sheldonian Theatre in Oxford, was inspired by illustrations in a book by Serlio of open air theatres like that of Marcellus in Rome. Although virtually all of Wren's work was in the Renaissance style he produced an architecture that was essentially his own and is clearly identifiable as such. The fact that he did not slavishly follow the style of Inigo Jones caused him problems with the Dean and Chapter of St Paul's Cathedral, London, and resulted in his having to compromise on some details, notably the inclusion of the balustrade at the top of the walls.

In the early eighteenth century it was common for young men of means to go on grand tours of Europe before 'settling down' and two such travellers were Lord Burlington and his friend William Kent who found delight in the work of Andrea Palladio while visiting Italy. On their return to Britain Lord Burlington commissioned William Kent to design a house for him in the Palladian style at Chiswick. The English publication in 1715 of Palladio's *The Four Books on Architecture* enabled Kent, Lord Burlington and others (notably Collen Campbell) to build according to the doctrine and principles laid down by Palladio.

The theory expounded by Palladio was basically that of a somewhat rigidly classical Roman style derived from his study of ancient buildings still standing in Italy and from the rigidly expressed principles on planning, proportions and details which were to be found in the writings of Vitruvius. These proportions and principles were rigidly applied to the Palladian buildings built in England between 1720 and 1760 and were reflected externally in monumental form in the central blocks of large country residences which contained portico, hall and salon. The blocks were balanced by wings containing kitchens and stables enabling the maintenance of the all important balance and symmetry. Ornament was restrained but what there was was quite elaborate and took the form of columns, pilasters, friezes and pediments based upon classical Renaissance detail. These buildings were seen as being appropriate to the educated class that was proud of its knowledge of Latin culture.

For almost forty years Palladianism was the fashion manifesting itself, not only in mansions for the wealthy but also in the pattern books which were to form the basis of many smaller houses in London and other cities in Britain and North America. The austere, symmetrical, almost forced, style was to be seen in buildings of all types.

By the 1760s Palladianism had given way to a new style, 'Neo-classicism' or 'Adam' as it is sometimes called (after Robert Adam the architect who fathered the style). Neo-classicism, as the name implies, was based upon a wider source of inspiration than that of one man in Renaissance Italy. The Neo-classicists took account of classical Roman buildings in Italy, Dalmatia and Syria and extended this to include Graeco-Roman decorative art as found at Pompeii and Herculaneum as well as the genuine Greek architecture of Southern Italy and Greece.

The nineteenth century

As the nineteenth century dawned we see a number of books being available including William Wilkins' *Antiquities of Magna Graecia* published in 1806. These books depicted buildings from the older civilizations that were to form the basis of 'the battle of the styles' in the nineteenth century.

Despite the vast output of building work in the nineteenth century —the transport, material production and technological changes which took place—no coherent design theory emerged. The debate tended to be very much on 'style' and we find buildings from that era clothed in Greek, Roman, Indian, Egyptian, and Gothic styles. Even writers like Pugin showed favour towards one style.

Probably the first true 'theory', covering both doctrine and principle, to emerge since Palladianism was that expounded by the Arts and Crafts movement led by William Morris. The members of the Arts and Crafts movement were rather displeased with the high Victorian buildings and designs that they saw all around them and they yearned for the hand-worked simplicity of earlier periods. In architecture they were drawn to the traditional vernacular rather than the heavily stylistic work that was prevalent at that time. The Arts and Crafts designers were concerned that their products should be well made, reflect a true use of natural materials and be completely free of any sham ornamentation. They totally rejected the mass production that epitomized the industrial revolution.

In architecture their work was an important milestone on the route to the 'modern' architecture of the second and third quarters of the twentieth century. The first building to be constructed that consciously reflected this theory was The Red House at Bexley, Kent, built by Philip Webb for William Morris himself. It is a large rambling building in warm hand-made red brick with a hand-made clay tile roof; other natural materials such as timber are also incorporated. Between 1860 and 1910 the Arts and Crafts movement continued in most western countries. In Britain the main Arts and Crafts architects were C. F. A. Voysey (1857–1941), M. H. Baillie-Scott (1865–1945), and C. R. Mackintosh (1868–1928), although the theories influenced many other architects of their day, notably R. Norman Shaw (1831–1912).

At the same time as this there was also another movement whose style has been described as Art Nouveau. The principles of Art Nouveau had many similarities with those of the Arts and Crafts movement but Art Nouveau differed in that it was very stylistic; the sinuous curves are readily identifiable. Art Nouveau was much more popular in France than it was in Britain and can best be appreciated in the metro stations of Paris by H. Guimard (1867–1942).

1900–1970

The debate about a simpler architecture, which reflected the technology of the twentieth century and the manufactured materials that were becoming available (notably steel and glass) had already begun before the outbreak of World War I. In Germany the first buildings that could be described as 'modern' in the now accepted sense had already been built: the AEG factory in Berlin 1908/9 by Peter Behrens and the more typical Fagus factory at Alfeld-en-der-Leine (1911/14) by Walter Gropius. In America it was Louis Sullivan (1856–1924) who first broke the mould of traditional nineteenth-century architecture. Sullivan has been credited with the expression 'form follows function' and it is probably on the theory behind this simple statement more than any other that the architecture of the twentieth century (or at least the best of it) rests. Sullivan's first building, as generally recognized, is the Guaranty Building, Buffalo, NY (1894/5) which was carried out whilst he was in the partnership of Adler and Sullivan. The Guaranty Building is an early skyscraper (of twelve stories) which was dependent upon the new technology, because without lifts, electric pumps, artificial ventilation, the telephone, and the steel frame there could have been no skyscrapers. Once the new technology was accepted it was logical that theories should develop that would reflect this. However, Sullivan's buildings are not devoid of ornament, indeed the original ornament of many of Sullivan's buildings is a superb art form in itself—in particular the cast iron detailing over the corner entrance of Sullivan's last major commercial project, the Carson, Pirie & Scott Department Store in Chicago 1899–1904.

Sullivan's famous pupil, Frank Lloyd Wright (1867–1959) developed Sullivan's idea of an organic architecture to include continuity of space, environmental harmony, unity of all parts of the design, and a truthful expression of materials, workmanship, and structure. Wright's principles had much in common with the Arts and Crafts movement in Britain. His early works—such as the prairie house in the suburbs of Chicago—are superb examples of architecture. They fully reflect these principles in every respect. Although Wright's first house—the Winslow house, River Forest, Illinois—was built in 1893, probably the finest of his early houses is the Robie House, Chicago of 1909 (see Plate 9). Wright was to continue building in his unique style throughout the first sixty years of the twentieth century, his final work—the Guggenheim Museum in New York—being completed in 1959. With the exception, perhaps, of Le Corbusier no twentieth century architect has had more influence on the architecture of his era than Frank Lloyd Wright. Had Wright been followed more than Le Corbusier in the years after World War II we may well have inherited a finer architecture.

The economic situations that prevailed at the end of World War I, and lasted well into the 1920s in most countries, resulted in little building activity. New political ideas emerging at that time meant that many of the promising young architects had to resort to writing and the preparation of utopian schemes. This naturally meant that a large number of theories abounded including Expressionism, which although mainly manifested in painting and literature, did appear to a limited extent in architecture and reflected the turbulent and restless desire to introduce change that was prevalent at that time. Expressionist theory sought to break up form into its component pieces in order to try to discover behind the pieces some sense that would bring freedom, happiness, and peace. Very few buildings were erected that can be described as expressionist. However, two are worthy of mention, namely Eric Mendelsohn's Einstein tower observatory at Potsdam (1921) and Hans Polzig's GrossesSchauspielhaus in Berlin (1919). However, in Holland at this time there was some very fine work which was a mixture of Arts and Crafts and Expressionism such, as J. F. Staal's Park Meerwijk colony (1918).

Other theories being put forward at this time were Neo-plasticism, De Stijl and Functionalism in Holland which was a leading force in architecture between 1917 and 1925 influenced greatly by Frank Lloyd Wright. Constructivism had its origins in post-revolution Russia and developed in Europe in the early 1920s.

In 1925 Walter Gropius published *International Architektur* which represented Gropius's assessment of what the New Objectivity (as it came to be known) in architecture was all about. The book presents the consistent view that future architecture would take the form of the white cubic box with set-backs in the plan and elevation, a form that was to become international (in fact, the International Style). The book took full account of the new technology—especially reinforced concrete which, although available from the middle of the nineteenth century only made its impact felt in architecture to any extent from after the end of World War I. The buildings were also expected to express their function and the design was to be a true reflection of that function: Sullivan's 'form follows function' again presenting itself.

One of the most influential books on the theory of architecture to be produced in the twentieth century was Le Corbusier's *Vers Une Architecture* (*Towards a New Architecture*) published in Paris in 1923—with an English translation in 1927. The importance of this book can best be emphasized by quoting the publisher's preface to the 1946 edition:

> This book has probably had as great an influence on English architectural thought as any one publication of the last fifty years. It first introduced the writings of Le Corbusier to the English reading public and was the first popular exposition in English of that 'modern movement' in architecture which was gradually establishing itself on the Continent of Europe during the first quarter of this century and to which England was to make her own powerful contribution during the 'thirties. Of this movement Le Corbusier was—and still is—one of the principal prophets.

Le Corbusier was impressed by the work of the engineer, which he saw being the result of the 'law of economy and governed by mathematical calculation'. He found satisfaction in the designs of strictly utilitarian structures such as grain silos and in the design of motor cars, ocean liners (then in their heyday) and the aeroplane (then very much in its infancy). It was when discussing the latter that he used his famous phrase 'a house is a machine for living in'. Le Corbusier sought simplicity and order in his design and totally rejected the concept of 'style'. He suggested the concept of raising buildings on 'pilotis' or columns to allow the ground to flow underneath and to free the site for vehicular movement; he also favoured using the roof area for outdoor living. By means of these two features he saw a positive gain of space—in fact equal to the site cover of the building. The concept of raising buildings on stilts is not new; it was used in many parts of the world to protect dwellings and their inhabitants from flood, wild animals or marauders. In parts of northern Australia, especially Queensland, the house raised on stilts or 'high house' as it is called remained popular for many years even in areas well away from 'flood' because of the advantages of extra space and the trapping of welcome cooling breezes as well as the ease of inspection against termite attack which the stilts provided. On buildings like Le Corbusier's Villa Savoie at Poissy, France (1928/9) the pilotis and roof garden concept work extremely well and even on his much later Unite d'Habitation in Marseilles (1946/52) the concept appears to be useful. However, the translation to British public sector housing of the 1950s and early 1960s was less than happy. What may well have been acceptable to sunny Marseilles and which worked moderately well at Roehampton on the edge of Richmond Park, Greater London, did not work in the wind-swept, bleak, grey areas of East London.

The International style and the ideas of Le Corbusier were to dominate architectural thought and teaching, with few exceptions, until the late 1960s. The resultant style of building became known as 'modern' and gradually became less than welcome in many quarters. After the destruction of World War II this modern style with its implication of a better world was almost universally seen as being the solution to all pre-war problems. By the mid-1960s doubts were being voiced at the destruction of many old familiar buildings and the replacement with new buildings which were not always well received. The 'modern' buildings often showed little respect for their surroundings and were truly 'international'. Buildings which looked much the same were being built in Birmingham and Brisbane, Stockholm and Singapore.

Contemporary

In 1968 a high rise block of flats in East London partially collapsed following a gas explosion in one of the flats. The block was called Ronan Point and with that collapse went much of the confidence in this new style and the doctrine and principles that lay behind it. The collapse of faith in this style of building really had little to do with the physical building collapse but it was probably the spark that ignited the fuse. In other parts of the world the disenchantment was also growing and in 1972 the award-winning flat development of Pruitt-Igoe, St Louis, USA was blown up; an event which has been described as 'the end of modernism'. Out of this disenchantment new ideas started to emerge. We now hear buildings described as being in the style of 'high-tech', 'Post-modernism', 'Neo-vernacular' and even once again 'Historicism'. Linked with all these at this time must also be the principles propounded by the conservation lobby (see Chapter 8).

'High-tech' really describes an architecture based on the exploitation of the elements of high technology and expressing these in the

Plate 1   Sainsbury Centre for Visual Arts, Norwich 1978 (Foster Associates).

form, shape and ornament of the building. High-tech has its roots in the industrial, transport, and exhibition buildings of the latter part of the nineteenth and the early twentieth centuries. High-tech has been most successful when applied to buildings of this type, for example the Centre Beaubourg in Paris, 1977 by Richard Rogers and Renzo Piano (see Plate 15), where giant trusses are exposed and the services that run on the outside of the building are painted in bright primary colours, and at the Sainsbury Centre for Visual Arts in Norwich (1978) by Norman Foster (see Plate 1). Attempts to use this theory for housing have been less successful—who really wants to live in a factory?

Post-modern architecture really encompasses both Neo-vernacular and Historicism both of which are discussed later. Although the term 'Post-modern' was first used in about 1948 it was not until the 1970s that we saw any real breakthrough into recognizable principles. Nevertheless it has been asserted that Antonio Gaudi (1852–1926) could be considered one of the first post-modernists in principle and practice despite the fact that he was, in strictly chronological terms, a pre-modernist (see Plate 22).

Post-modern architecture is trying to say something to both the trained designer and the layman in much the same way as classical or Gothic architecture. There, the form and shape spoke to the trained eye whilst the ornament and sculpture which were integral parts of the structure were able to be related to by the layman.

Plate 2 *Hillingdon Civic Centre, Greater London, 1977 (Robert Matthew, Johnson & Partners). Photo courtesy of: Robert Matthew, Johnson & Partners.*

Plate 3 *Housing at Ingatestone, Essex, 1978 for Countryside Homes PLC (David Ruffle Associates). Photo courtesy of: David Ruffle Associates, photographer Sam Lambert Partnership.*

Plate 4 (left)   House at Dedham, Essex, 1972 (Erith & Terry). Photo courtesy of: Erith & Terry.

Plate 5 (right)   'Spec' builders 'mock' Georgian house, Greater London, c.1980.

   The Neo-vernacular branch of Post-modernism has its roots, as its name implies, in traditional, local, small buildings which were mainly domestic but which could also include basic farm buildings such as stables and barns and even small simple chapels. Most Neo-vernacular work in Britain is found in housing, and some of the work is very successful indeed (see Plate 3). More massive buildings have also been attempted in this style such as Hillingdon Civic Centre, Greater London (1974/7) by Andrew Derbyshire of Robert Matthew, Johnson, Marshall & Partners (see Plate 2). The publication in 1973 by Essex County Council of its excellent work *A Design Guide for Residential Areas* has resulted in much Essex Neo-vernacular being used throughout Britain, which was far removed from the intentions of the authors of this guide.
   Historicism as a form of building has, of course, never totally died out—some designers have continued with fully historical styles throughout the twentieth century amid much criticism. Generally speaking, however, such buildings have proved popular with laymen. Historicism can embody any of the previous styles and principles of

Plate 6   Nursery, Covent Garden, Greater London, 1981 (Terry Farrell Partnership).

the past with the most popular tending to be Neo-classical and, in Britain, Neo-Georgian. It is not necessary for a building in historicist style to be a true replica of the earlier style; it could use the historic elements correctly and extend the tradition to relate to the function, technology and other constraints of the project. It is absolutely vital that any designer adopting a historicist style must fully understand the origins of that style.

The work of the late Raymond Erith, whose tradition is being kept alive by Quinlan Terry in Britain, reflects a thorough understanding of the Georgian tradition in English architecture. Quinlan Terry's small house (see Plate 4) embodying his seven characteristics of classical architecture (namely: a symmetrical plan; a front door in the middle; windows the right place and of the correct size and proportion; a simple pitched roof; materials that are both traditional and loadbearing and some central vestige of the classical orders) can be contrasted with the 'mock-Georgian' of much speculative housing where neither the proportions nor the detailing of the source are appreciated (see Plate 5).

14

Not all designers who employ a historical approach use so strict a theory as Quinlan Terry. Robert Venturi maintains that his use of history is to provide a source of general lessons about space, form, and texture rather than as a storehouse of symbols and image.

In Britain the Terry Farrell Partnership's Nursery in Covent Garden, Greater London (see Plate 6) follows this principle and can be contrasted with the design by Quinlan Terry of a Summerhouse shown in Plate 7 which follows the stricter historical approach.

Conclusion

In the next two decades it will be interesting to see whether these styles merge, develop in parallel or give way to yet more styles and eventually to a style that will be readily identifiable with the latter years of the twentieth century. Maybe we will have a re-run of the nineteenth century 'battle of the styles'.

Plate 7   Design for a summerhouse, Northants, 1982 (Erith & Terry). Photo courtesy of: Erith & Terry.

References

Essex County Council *A Design Guide for Residential Areas* (Essex County Council, 1973).

Gropius, W. *International Architektur*, 1925.

Jencks, C. A. *The Language of Post-Modern Architecture* (Academy: London, 1978).

Little, B. *English Historic Architecture* (Batsford, London: 1964).

Le Corbusier *Towards a New Architecture* (Architectural Press: London, 1974).

Open University, The, A305 *History of Architecture and Design 1890–1939* (The Open University Press: Milton Keynes, 1975).

Palladio, A. *Four Books on Architecture* (Dover: London, 1965).

Vitrivius, *The Ten Books on Architecture* (Constable: London, 1960).

2

The design process

Introduction

The design process must be seen as a decision-making process—we are constantly making decisions, consciously or unconsciously, which affect our life or our immediate environment and when we come to design something we are only extending this decision-making process in a more systematic way.

Historical developments

The actual design process for buildings has remained basically unchanged throughout history. However, the method and implementation has changed significantly. When the human race first started to provide some form of shelter for itself and its possessions these early pioneers had to look around for suitable materials to use—and these all had to be obtained within the immediate locality of the building. With these simple materials—branches, leaves, animal skins and stones—a crude shelter was fashioned. In order to be a success certain performance requirements had be to solved: firstly the shelter had to be a climatic modifier (it had to keep out the rain and snow and to form protection from the wind and perhaps the sun); it had to be high enough for the occupier to stand upright in most of it; and it had to be stable enough not to fall down or be able to be knocked down easily. The design method was really one of trial and error—if the first shelter fell down the next was built stronger, if it leaked or flooded a change in technique was adopted.

Gradually a conventional style of shelter became the norm in a particular locality—certain materials, techniques and arrangements became accepted as correct. Decisions still had to be made by the 'designer' but these tended to relate to location, size and choosing from among two or more ways of solving a particular problem.

As new skills and tools were developed, new materials were used (or existing materials were used in a more sophisticated way). However, there was a tendency to design in these 'new' materials in the same way as had been done with the old, (for example, when the ancient Egyptians first built columns in stone they followed the same form as the bundles of reeds used previously even to the extent of using the leaf and flower motif for the capital). The Greeks copied their earlier post and beam timber structures when they started building in stone. Nearer our time the great Victorian engineers provided decorated capitals to the cast iron columns that supported the roofs of the glass-roofed train sheds. These capitals usually incorporated leaf motifs.

Until the Renaissance period most buildings followed this analogous style and thus the design method could be seen as being evolutionary, with no single person doing the 'designing'. The 'client' might say to the builder that he wanted a new house built on his land similar to a recently built neighbour's house but in stone rather than timber; he would like an extra space where he and his wife could sleep as he had seen at another house. As work proceeded other decisions would be made, ideas would be floated by various people (generally based on existing knowledge, but occasionally a new idea) and these would be considered and accepted or rejected. Finally a new house would be completed and tested. (Was it warm? Did it leak? Did the fire draw properly?) From the testing a pool of knowledge was built up and passed on.

As the Renaissance developed and became the accepted style of building a further development in the design method took place. The building designs of the Renaissance period were based on certain rules which had originally been developed by the ancient Greeks and Romans and rediscovered in the fourteenth and fifteenth centuries. This new style was introduced into Britain in the latter part of the sixteenth century and by the time of the Restoration it had become the accepted style. As building layouts were therefore now much more geometrical, and often also symmetrical, it became necessary to test ideas before building work started and this led to a much greater use of drawings. This was also the point when there began to be a distinct separation between the person who designed and the person who built; a factor that was eventually to lead to the development of separate professions.

The current situation

The use of hand-drawn drawings remains the dominant design

method today although models have always been a supplementary way of displaying the final scheme to the client and in recent years to planning authorities as well as the general public. Models are not new; Christopher Wren produced models of his designs for St Paul's Cathedral in London.

Computers are now becoming increasingly important as an aid to the design process (see p. 27) and they will probably revolutionize the design method in the near future as much as drawings did in earlier times.

Today, as in the past, there are many 'gifted' designers but even they must design in a logical way following the time-honoured process. In addition to this a much more scientific approach is needed nowadays; buildings have more rigorous performance standards and there is a growing realization that buildings and the built environment have an important part to play in a person's behaviour patterns. Our range of materials and techniques is vast and our knowledge of what is going on elsewhere can be instantaneous. In the past a designer had to rely on a sketch of a building located in another city that he was unable to visit. The sketch would often be poor and in most cases would only show one view. Nowadays the television camera can capture a building in three dimensions and from every aspect so that, for example, there are few people in Britain with any interest in buildings who do not know what the Sydney Opera House looks like and what its setting is, although few will have actually been fortunate enough to experience this building *in situ*.

The five phases

The design process can be considered in five phases: brief; analysis; synthesis; implementation; and verification. However, it must not be seen as a linear process but rather as a circular one as it is also a continuous process with each phase overlapping the other. Some phases and sub-phases have to be pursued in parallel and many will have to be repeated. There should be feedback at all phases wherever this is possible.

Brief

The first phase is that of the brief. In some cases a very comprehensive brief will be provided by the client whilst in other cases the brief will simply state his requirements in the simplest form (e.g. a three-bedroomed house with an *en suite* bathroom and a separate dining room). In most cases, however, the brief will be neither comprehensive nor minimal—it will give a reasonable amount of information but it will not be able to form the basis of the design without further work.

Basically the brief should clarify the clients requirements. The designer will need to have a full and thorough understanding of the problems and also of the client's wishes. It is necessary to have an appreciation of the philosophy of the client with regard to the building and also to see his priorities. Most, if not all, building designs are compromises and it is therefore necessary to be able to rank a client's requirements so that one does not sacrifice the principal elements. For some clients (initial) cost may be the over-riding factor; this is often the case for local and national government and, unfortunately, rarely results in a good building. Ease of maintenance, flexibility, high standard of visual quality or minimum energy consumption could easily be the major factor around which other requirements may have to be compromised or even sacrificed.

The brief needs to contain a statement on the function of the building—it is better to say that a house is required by a married couple in their late thirties with two teenage children (girl, aged 17 studying for university entrance and a boy, aged 16 already working in the local supermarket) than to say that a three-bedroomed house is required. Unfortunately, in too many cases the final user of the building is not the client and therefore the statement of function is very bland. In the early 1960s in Britain the government set up a committee under the chairmanship of Sir Parker Morris to produce a guide for the design of local authority housing. This guide *Homes for Today and Tomorrow*, better known as the *Parker Morris Standards*, became a key component of the brief for local authority and housing association houses in Britain until 1980. Unfortunately, the design team also had to grapple with 'housing cost yardsticks' for most of this time and many problems resulted in trying to resolve these two almost unresolvable requirements.

In recent years there have been a number of interesting developments in Britain of 'community architecture' where the final users of the buildings are brought into the design team at the very beginning and make a positive contribution to the design process.

It can, therefore, be seen that the brief should contain much more than a mere schedule of accommodation. A good brief should include something on the desired appearance of the building(s) including the range of materials that is preferred. In many cases the local planning authority may well have a say (which can vary from limited to extensive in these matters). In this respect the client's views may not be paramount and thus changes in the brief may well have to take place. The brief may also include a statement on the method of construction to be employed—this is more likely to be the case where a client has a background of previous building. Average clients are not likely to concern themselves with construction although they may ask the design team to avoid certain materials or to design for low maintenance or flexibility—all of which will have a bearing on construction.

Cost will invariably be a big factor in the client's mind and this may be stated at the outset with a rigid upper limit. Alternatively the design team's advice may be sought. On many projects, particularly those of comprehensive or complex nature a cost consultant or quantity surveyor will form part of the design team and following from their advice the brief may need to be recast. Lower initial costs usually mean higher maintenance costs and this should be stressed at an early stage.

There may well be other important factors in the brief, such as ensuring that the existing use of the building on the site is not interrupted or that time is of the essence (as in the case of an exhibition stand which must be complete in time for the exhibition or sporting facilities which must be ready for, perhaps, the Olympic Games).

A good brief will be prepared by both the design team and client working together. This is not always possible as in the case of a competition but, even then, there is invariably a date by which questions must be submitted and the answers to these are circulated to all contestants thus enabling the next step to take place which is that of clarification of the brief.

The design team not only has to clarify the brief but it also has to develop it and this can involve considerable research to find the information required. Take, for example, a recreation hall. The client may ask for a multi-purpose hall to accommodate (say) 250 persons at a concert or film show, the hall also being used for badminton, country dancing and numerous other purposes. The design team will have to research the spatial requirements of 250 persons seated and also those of badminton as well as ancillary toilet and changing facilities. Some information such as that cited above is readily available whilst some, especially for extremely specialised or new uses, may need considerable research. Once the brief is finalized the analysis stage may be embarked upon.

Analysis

This is the stage of the process where the design team starts to break down the problems into its various parts and then into its sub-parts. The problem has to be explored in a comprehensive way and the design team will use every means at its disposal to do this. The problem should be examined intellectually by means of logical processes of induction and deduction; it should be examined imaginatively by contemplating the range of possibilities and, of course, it should be analysed using all the modes of visual analysis available to the designer such as sketches, diagrams and models.

Wherever it is possible the problem should be reduced to quantifiable terms. It should then be possible to examine the problem comparatively by reference to the design team's own experience as well as that of other design teams through case studies.

It is usually possible to break down the problem into three basic parts:

  (i) planning;
 (ii) constraints including materials and construction; and
(iii) aesthetics.

It must be stressed that each of these parts cannot be dealt with in isolation as they are very much inter-related. For example, the aesthetics of the building will depend very much upon the materials used and also upon the construction whilst the construction will, in turn, depend upon the plan form of the building where wide open spaces will require a different construction from many small spaces which can be separated by load bearing partitions.

From this analysis a vast amount of data will start to accumulate and it will be necessary for the design team to sort it out, together with the specialized data that its research will have provided. At this stage it may well be found that more data is required or that the brief requires modifications, especially if there are conflicting requirements such as too much space and/or equipment being demanded for the budget allowance. It may be felt that the problem is insoluble as it stands and decisions will have to be made on what has to be sacrificed.

Finally, it should be possible to state the problem in such a way that it is capable of being solved, with the ultimate aim being agreed upon by all parties who must be confident of a successful completion. It is now possible to move onto the synthesis stage.

Synthesis

Solutions to the problems will probably have started to suggest themselves in the previous stages. However, this is the main creative part of the whole design process. Much of the activity will be unconscious and may well take place away from the drawing board or computer.

The creative stage of the design process has therefore now begun. The design team will start by working from the general to the particular. For most designers sketches, mainly freehand, will be the principal medium for this initial work. As solutions start to present themselves it will be necessary to assess these solutions against the criteria of the brief and the whole host of other influences on the building which are described later in this book. In many cases this will result in the solution being rejected and the synthesis stage will have to commence again, in other cases it may be necessary to revert once more to the analysis stage.

Gradually it will become apparent that one particular solution appears to be better than others and this is the one that will probably be developed after the next stage, which is that of verification.

Verification

This is the stage of proving and improving the solution, to show that the solution is valid in every way. Every part of the design must be tested and must be seen to be valid. Some parts of the design are easy to test such as the construction and the materials, the legislative controls, the behaviour as a climatic modifier, and the economic viability; others are more difficult to assess objectively such as the workability of the scheme. Will the space allocations be correct and will the circulation work? In particular, the appearance of the building will have to be judged at this stage. How will it fit into its surroundings? Is it 'right' for its purpose?

This stage of verification is difficult and must never be overlooked. Wherever possible the design must be judged objectively but where this is not possible subjective verification is necessary and this should not be restricted to the design team; the office 'crit' is a good way of obtaining the valuable opinion of others.

The design team will wish to use every aid possible at this verification stage from past experience to the computer. The latter is particularly useful for checking such things as energy efficiency, daylight and sunlight as well as checking the appearance of the building, both externally and internally, from many angles (see p. oo). Once the design has been verified and found to be satisfactory in all respects it is possible to move on to the implementation stage.

Implementation

It is now possible to commence the preparation of the design in its final form. Detailed sketch drawings can now be produced which will enable the client and other interested parties to appreciate the final design. Figure 1 shows sketches for two houses to be built in an outer London suburb in the form that they would be submitted to the local planning authority for detailed planning consent.

In some cases a model may be the best way of depicting a final scheme especially where the project is large and complex, on a sensitive site, for a building of great importance or, perhaps, for a building which will require public subscription.

Sketches and even models can be misleading if they are drawn or, in the case of models, viewed from the wrong angle—from a viewpoint that will not be possible in true life. Models are often viewed from above—a vantage point rare for most completed buildings. Sketches often look superb showing little traffic and an abundance of flower troughs and bright umbrellas, but the reality may well be different.

A further stage of the implementation process is the production of all the drawings and documentation necessary to get the building built together with all the host of approvals which are nowadays mandatory, the appointment of the contractor and the actual construction of the building. It is important that this part of the implementation process is not separated from the design process because unless the single-minded approach continues through this stage some, or all, of the original inspiration may be lost. Too many potentially fine buildings have been ruined during this stage by the lack of continuity in design philosophy. Sometimes the design team loses interest, someone else takes over the leadership or the client continually changes his brief throughout the project; all, or any of these factors can result in disillusionment and a resultant poor quality building.

It may be worth stressing here that one of the constant problems for the designer is the client changing his mind and hence the brief. There is no hard and fast rule as to where the point of no return comes in the design of a building beyond which there should be no changes in the brief but really there should be no changes once the analysis stage is under way. This, however, is unrealistic and probably the only thing that can be done is for the design team to spend as much time as possible with the client at the brief stage to ensure that this is as comprehensive as possible.

The client should be made aware that any changes thereafter may require a return to the brief stage with the consequent increase in cost

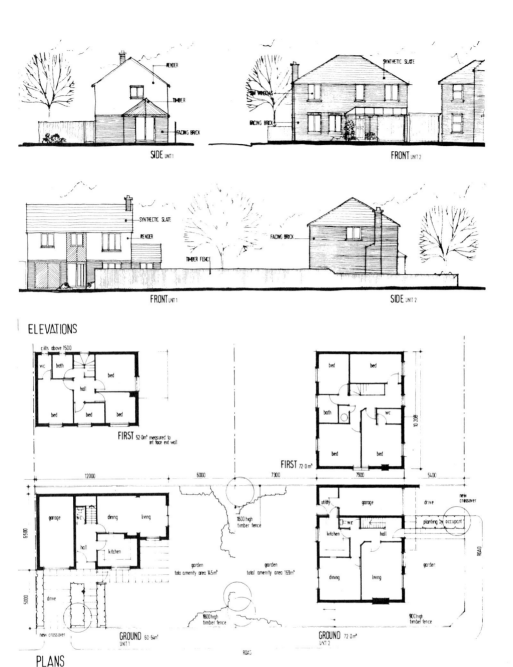

ELEVATIONS

PLANS

Figure 1   Sketches for two houses to be built in an outer London suburb in the form that they would be submitted to the local planning authority for detailed planning consent (a location plan should also be included). Architect: Geoff Mules BArch, Msc, RIBA). Drawings courtesy of Geoff Mules.

and delay. This may be a little too utopian and maybe it is necessary to accept that most design teams will suffer from their client's change of mind.

Feedback

The final stage in the design process and that which is all too often ignored is that of feedback. The main problem with regard to this aspect of the design stage is the length of time that occurs between the initial decision to build and the completion and occupation of a building. Even once the building is in use a period of time must pass before a thoroughly objective view of the work can be made. In the meantime the members of the design team will probably have designed many other buildings and the real benefit of any feedback from a building designed many years before may well be of limited value. Nevertheless wherever possible the design team should obtain as much feedback as it can on earlier designs by all means available from observation to enquiry and questionnaires, the latter being processed, if necessary, by computer to obtain the necessary information.

It is common for buildings to be used by people who have little or no say in formulating the brief, as has already been mentioned, and it is often from these people that one must obtain the feedback. The London architect, Erno Goldfinger, made headline news when he went to live in a high-rise block of local authority flats that he had designed. His stay only lasted, as indeed was intended, for a few months. It is obvious that Mr Goldfinger learnt much about his design that he would otherwise not have done had he ignored this stage of the design process despite the fact that his lifestyle would, perhaps, have been much more suited to high-rise living than that of many of the local authority tenants.

More scientific methods of feedback are now available for testing such things as heat loss from buildings and these can prove to be very valuable for testing those aspects of the design that can be measured objectively during the verification stage. However, it is in those aspects that can only be judged subjectively that prove more difficult. In fact, on aesthetics, time, and fashion can change peoples' views quite substantially. St Paul's Cathedral in London has not always been thought of highly, whilst the buildings built in the 1950s which were to herald a brave new world were almost universally admired when they were completed (especially within the building professions). These are now rarely viewed with high esteem even within the building professions.

Computer-aided design

The advent of computers will, over the next few years, continue to have a very substantial impact on the design process as well as on the preparation of the documentation necessary for the production of a building.

In the design process the computer can be used to aid the formulation and analysis of the brief by simulation. For example, a programme can be developed of students arriving at a refectory over the peak luncheon period of say noon to 2.00 pm and can show the time taken for them to select their food, pay for same, eat, and depart. From this it will be possible to determine the length of the servery race, extent of queue space needed, number of cash desks, tables, and chairs, and even staff required.

During the synthesis stage the computer has only a limited application. This is the main generative stage of the process with so many solutions being possible for any given problems that the use of computers can become unmanageable. A window to a room is a good example. It would be possible to feed into the computer the daylight and ventilation requirements, maximum desirable heat loss or gain and type of window and to receive hundreds of suitable answers. To maximize computer potential the selection of the window would have to be made by the design team and its performance checked by the computer.

This brings us to the verification stage and this is where the computer is an extremely valuable tool. It enables the design to be checked in every way. The various spaces and rooms can be checked against the brief, for workability and special needs, and their acoustics, daylighting, ventilation, and energy consumption can be checked against recommended codes, regulations, and specific client requirements. Even the visual appearance of the rooms and spaces can be assessed by setting up numerous internal perspectives, something that would be so time-consuming to carry out manually that it would rarely, if ever, be done. The structure of the building and its construction cost can be checked as can the external appearance again by the use of prospectives.

It is at the implementation stage that the computer had been of most use to date. Considerable time and manpower savings can be effected by the design team in using the computer to produce the documentation necessary for a building. Drawings, specifications, bills of quantities, and schedules can all be produced quickly and accurately and, in addition, they can be amended easily and thoroughly which can be a very real problem where work is carried out manually. During the construction, phase management, and accounting tasks can be handled by computer whilst on commissioning such things as furniture schedules and the clients manual can be produced.

The computer can also assist at the feedback stage in analysing and processing information which is fed in and this will prove invaluable on future projects.

Conclusion

As the requirements and life of the human race have become more complex so too has the implementation of the design process and with it has been developed more valuable aids than have ever been available before. Nevertheless, the skill of the design team and their painstaking work throughout the design process are the principal factors determining the success or otherwise of the completed project. The traditional roles of the individual members of the team are tending to break down—or at least to cross one another's boundaries. It is essential that all members of the team must collaborate much more in the future if better buildings are to be the result.

References

Broadbent, G. and Ward, A. (eds) *Design Methods in Architecture* (Architectural Associates: London, 1969).

Gregory, S. A. (ed.) *The Design Method* (Butterworth: London, 1966).

Jones, J. C. *Design Methods; Seeds of Human Futures* (Wiley Interscience: Chichester, 1980).

Lawson, B. R. *How Designers Think* (Architectural Press: London, 1980).

MacKinder, M. *Design Decision-making in Architectural Practice* (B. R. E. Information Paper 11/82).

MacKinder, M. and Marvin, H. *Design Decision-making in Architectural Practice* (Institute of Advanced Architectural Studies, University of York, Research Paper 19, 1982).

Ministry of Housing and Local Government, Houses for Today and Tomorrow (the Parker Morris Standards), (HMSO: London, 1961).

Port, S. *Computer-aided Design for Engineers and Architects* (Granada: St Albans, 1984).

Reynolds, R. A. *Computer Methods for Architects* (Butterworth: London, 1980).

RIBA *Handbook of Architectural Practice and Management* (RIBA Publications: London, 1965).

3
Climatic influences

Introduction

The primary purpose of buildings throughout history has been to provide shelter for the occupants from the elements. It would be possible to muse that if there was somewhere in the world with a constant temperature of about 21° C and moderate relative humidity with moisture arriving to support human and animal life as well as crops by some means other than precipitation the human race would not have needed to build any form of shelter, but no such place exists and it would be a rather boring place to live in if it did.

As life became more complex a building not only had to provide shelter from the elements but it also had to provide security for its occupants from marauding animals and tribes and also had to provide a place of safe-keeping for the owners possessions. Thus the two basic requirements of a building—shelter and security—were born. Security is discussed in Chapter 6 and it is the purpose of this chapter to consider those requirements relating to shelter.

The form and construction of a building is dependent upon climate more than upon any other design factor, hence the great variety of built forms throughout the world. The climate of an area, together with the geological formation of that area, controls the availability and type of materials whilst the climate itself determines the degree and type of shelter required. The rate and quantity of precipitation invariably control the pitch of the roof whilst for covering the climate and geological nature controls the materials—thatch, stone slates, wood shingles etc.—which also control the pitch.

In recent years technology, in the form of 'new' materials and environmental services, have enabled designers to depart from the traditional methods and materials suited to the locality of the building. More recently the energy crisis of 1973 has prompted designers to re-consider dependence on fossil fuels for environmental control and also to look anew at some of the building materials that either represent a finite source or require much fossil fuel energy to produce. One material that has fared well under this scrutiny is timber, which although hungry of land and slow to produce from planting to harvesting, uses very little fossil-fuel produced energy except for its conversion and transportation. Timber is also regenerative over a long time span.

Human comfort

The environmental standards required within buildings are invariably controlled by those that result in maximum human comfort. There are occasions where some piece of sensitive machinery (e.g. some scientific equipment or the storage of goods as in a cold store) will take precedence but these are the exception rather than the rule.

The human body demands a fairly limited range of environmental conditions in order to maintain maximum comfort and efficiency. This range is considerably less than that found throughout the world or even throughout the year, or even day, in most parts of the world.

World climatic zones

The inhabited world can be broadly divided into three principal climatic zones, namely: tropical, temperate, and polar but within these there are very wide variations and such terms as sub-tropical, humid tropical and dry tropical, desert, Mediterranean, western sea-board, warm temperate, cool temperate, alpine are all used to describe climatic conditions applicable to certain parts of the world.

Many factors influence the climate of a particular place and even within a town or suburb there can be several different micro-climates. The factors that influence the climate of a particular locality are altitude, proximity of large areas of water, density of habitation, direction, frequency and speed of winds, proximity of hills, mountains and valleys, ground cover and planting, as well as the actual location in longitude and principally latitude. Generally for any given latitude the northern hemisphere is warmer than the southern hemisphere due to prevailing winds and the greater land mass in the northern hemisphere.

Because of the way in which the earth revolves the prevailing winds tend to be south-westerly and this is advantageous to western Europe and the west coast of North America from a temperature point of

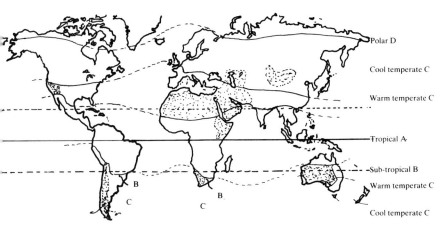

Polar D

Cool temperate C

Warm temperate C

Tropical A

Sub-tropical B

Warm temperate C

Cool temperate C

 Desert

Figure 2   World climatic zones (simplified version).

view although not necessarily from the point of view of dry summers. Figure 2 shows the principal climate zones of the world whilst Table 1 gives a broad summary of the impact the climate has on building design for each zone.

The climate of the United Kingdom

Many jokes are made about the climate of the United Kingdom but, for the most part, it is very favourable with the extremes of heat and cold experienced in many parts of the world being rare. Generally the rainfall is fairly regular, drought and flood conditions are infrequent as are blizzards and fierce thunderstorms.

The United Kingdom climate is classified as western sea-board and this is one of the sub-divisions within the temperate range. The prevailing wind over much of the country is south-westerly and this is the direction for about 70 per cent of the year. The south-westerly wind blows off the Atlantic and is therefore a rain-bearing wind, which is cool in summer and warm in winter. The rain-bearing nature of this wind results in the south west and west of the country being wetter than the east. Because the south of England is the closest part of the country to the equator it is understandable that this part of the country is the warmest and sunniest. Towns can also be up to 9° C warmer than the surrounding countryside, and London is therefore one of the warmest spots in Britain, especially in winter; this is mainly due to the densely packed buildings and vehicles all emitting warmth.

Because of its island nature no part of the United Kingdom is more than about 100 km from the sea which means that the air over the United Kingdom is fairly moist most of the time and thus relative humidity is moderately high. On hot days in summer this high humidity can make it seem even hotter especially if it is a still day.

When the wind blows from the eastern sector the weather of the United Kingdom undergoes a change. In winter, east winds tend to be very cold blowing as they do off the land mass of Europe; conversely in summer warm, dry and less humid weather usually results when an east wind blows—although from about Lincolnshire northwards the east coast is often very cool under these circumstances because the wind blows over the North Sea.

Much of England is fairly flat and thus topography plays little part in affecting the weather except for wind velocity in the eastern counties, but in the hillier parts of England and in other parts of the kingdom the hills and mountains play an important part in determining wind direction and velocity, precipitation and fog in any particular locality.

Impact of climate on building design

Sun

Apart from the psychological uplift that almost all of us enjoy when we see the sun shining it is a well-known fact that sunshine is an aid to cleanliness, that it has germicidal qualities (although these are no longer considered as important today as in the past), that it provides the body with vitamin E and that, of course, it is a source of warmth and the cheapest form of energy.

Such is the importance of sunshine in our buildings that the British Standards Institution issued a Draft for Development entitled *Basic Data for the Design of Buildings: Sunlight* in 1980 to replace the code of practice originally produced in 1945 (C.P.3 Chapter 1(B): 1945 Sunlight (houses, flats and schools only). This draft recommends that for dwellings 'a minimum standard of 3 hours of possible sunlight on 1 March be received on the plan of the inside face of the window wall at the centre of the window'. In assessing the amount of sunlight, any

Table 1   Summary of climatic conditions and major impact on building design.

Climatic conditions	Building design requirements
A Tropical	Buildings to be designed to maximize shading; cooling breezes; protection against heavy rainfall, typhoons, cyclones etc. No winter heating required except in upland areas; cooling required*; insect screening.
B Sub-tropical	Shading; cooling breezes; sun penetration in winter months; protection against hot winds; heavy rainfall, typhoons, cyclones etc. Some winter heating required; cooling desirable*; insect screening often required.
C Temperate	Sun penetration autumn, winter, spring, but shading in summer; protection against cold winds, rain, frost, and snow. Winter heating essential; summer cooling occasionally desirable*; some areas need insect screening.
D Polar	Sun penetration all year; protection against cold winds, snow and very low temperature; heating essential; no summer cooling required. Some areas need insect screening.
E Desert	Shading; sun penetration in winter months; protection against hot winds in summer, cold in winter; protection against dust infiltration; cooling essential*; insect screening essential; winter heating required.

* Summer cooling may be by efficiently designed natural means. Many societies have excellent traditional methods of achieving high levels of comfort within their buildings without resolving to air conditioning.

below the altitude of 5° should be discounted and account should be taken of local obstructions such as balcony or roof overhangs. However, although this is a good guide it should be treated as a minimum.

In the northern hemisphere the sun apparently travels around the south on its route from east to west and thus from a sunlight point of view a southerly aspect is the most desirable. During the summer months the sun is at a higher angle at noon than it is in the winter and it is easy to calculate the angle of the sun and its penetration for any particular place using sun path diagrams or by computer.

The penetration of sunlight into rooms and spaces can be desired at differing times of the day which is indeed fortunate to the designer. In domestic buildings morning sun is desirable in kitchens and bedrooms whilst afternoon sun is seen as being more beneficial in living rooms. To achieve this kitchens and bedrooms should be located on the east whilst living rooms should be on the west or south. South-facing bedrooms are acceptable in winter but can get uncomfortably warm in the summer and as the sun, in the summer, rises north of east it is fairly late before a south-facing bedroom gets sunlight from early May until August. South- or west-facing kitchens can become unbearably warm on summer afternoons and early evenings when the evening meal is being prepared.

East-facing work places are desirable as this permits the office or other work place to warm up before workers arrive presenting a bright cheery atmosphere which is also warm for the start of the day; west- and south-facing offices can become very hot and uncomfortable in the summer months unless there is proper shading of the windows.

Unfortunately the sunshine cycle does not follow the temperature cycle and this can pose problems of sunlight control. The warmest day of the year is supposed to be roughly four to six weeks after the longest day (22 June) whist the coldest day follows the shortest day by a similar time (as the days lengthen the cold strengthens). Thus on, say, 22 May it is usually desirable to have as much sunshine penetrating buildings as possible whilst when the sun is at the same altitude on 22 July one may wish to exclude most of the sunshine. The temperature cycle is even more noticeable when one compares the 22 September (usually still quite warm) with the 22 March which is often still very wintery with snow not by any means unknown even in the South of England. This difference means that all forms of sunlight control need to be adjustable and if one is trying to keep the heat of the sun out then sunlight control must be on the outside of the glass to prevent the heat rays from entering the building. One very effective form of sunlight control which actually follows the temperature cycle rather than the sunlight cycle is the deciduous tree—this is invariably bare until late April and the density of leaves increases to reach the maximum about August. The first leaves start to fall early October with the tree becoming bare about the beginning of December. Thus carefully selecting deciduous trees can be very useful as shading devices (see also the section on aspect in Chapter 4).

Not all spaces and uses welcome the sunshine and in these cases either north-facing windows should be provided or, less satisfactorily, windows on other aspects should be permanently shaded. North light is a very constant light and is desirable in places such as artists' studios and factories—indeed the term 'north-light' has been given to the saw-tooth roof form incorporating glazing often found in buildings of this type. In hospitals sun should not fall on the patient's face whilst he or she is lying in bed at any time of the year and to this

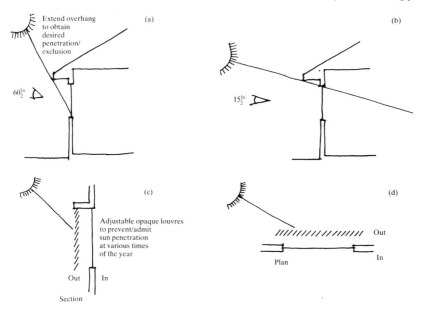

Figure 3 Sunshine penetration and control: (a) south aspect, London, 22 June; (b) south aspect, London, 22 December; (c) south aspect horizontal louvres; (d) east/west aspect, vertical louvres.

extent sun-patches should be calculated to ensure that this inconvenience does not occur. Figure 3 shows examples of sunshine penetration and controls for buildings.

Since the energy crisis of 1973 attention has turned more and more to alternative energy sources other than the fossil fuels. As has been mentioned earlier sun is the cheapest source of energy and the only problem and expense comes in trying to harness it. Much research has gone on in recent years on this matter and a number of experimental solar houses and other buildings have been built in the United Kingdom and elsewhere. Solar power has possibilities in the United Kingdom for initial heating of water for hot water and space heating but there are still many problems that have to be resolved before its use is likely to be widespread. However, the possibilities are there and the design team needs to consider them if it is to produce a building that is going to employ solar heating. Area of wall/roof space at the correct angle and facing the proper direction is necessary together with adequate provision for heat storage.

Even where there is no intention to employ solar collectors much can be done to reduce the heating load on buildings by carefully planning rooms and spaces to optimize sunlight and to reduce the effects of cold winds. Plate 8 shows a design for a house in Milton Keynes which maximizes the use of sunlight. Figure 4 shows a conventional design for a north/south UK aspect which the Building Research Establishment claim to use between 25 per cent and 50 per cent of the normal energy requirement of a similar house.

With the more conscious attempts that are now being made in Britain to reduce the heat load on buildings during the winter months and to maximize the warming effects of the sun problems can arise due to overheating in the summer months. Little attempt has been made in the past in Britain to reduce the solar gains in buildings during the summer months. This was probably not only because the climate of these islands is generally not hot enough to warrant such concern but also because the buildings did not hitherto maximize the heating effects of the sun in winter and therefore were not subject to overheating in the summer. The poor insulating and draught proofing qualities of most older buildings especially in the domestic sphere,

Plate 8   House at Milton Keynes, Bucks 1979 (Solar Energy Developments). Photo courtesy of: Milton Keynes Development Corporation.

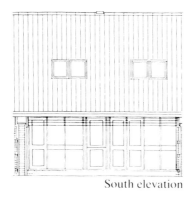

South elevation

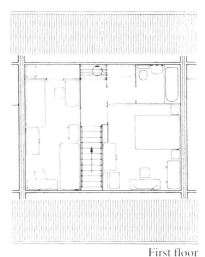

Ground floor

First floor

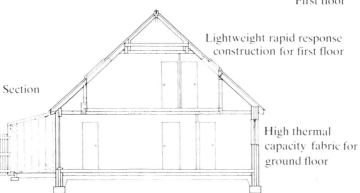

Section

Lightweight rapid response construction for first floor

High thermal capacity fabric for ground floor

Figure 4 One of several conventionally designed energy-efficient houses designed by the Building Research Establishment, Watford, Herts. Drawing courtesy of: Building Research Establishment.

allowed any daytime heat build up in summer to escape quickly at night thus producing a comfortable environment for sleeping which is the time most people require a lower temperature.

Buildings designed to maximize the sun's heating in winter and to cool very slowly will react similarly in summer unless special care is taken in the design to reduce the heating effect of the sun at that time of the year. Thus the design team must now be as conscious of heat gain in summer in a cool temperate climate, like Britain, as they always have been in the warmer parts of the world.

Designers must also consider the problem of glare which results when a view of the sun lies within 45° of the line of sight. This can be checked from drawings in conjunction with sunpath diagrams. In addition consideration should be given to glare which can result from the reflection of the sun from bright reflective surfaces such as bodies of water and other buildings as well as the area of sky that is visible. Glare can be worse when there is a film of thin cloud over the sky than when there is a cloudless sky. In addition, small windows in dark walls can often result in unpleasant glare because of the contrast between the window and wall surface.

Wind

The influence of wind on perceived temperature and body comfort is very important. In some parts of the world weather forecasts include, in winter, a chill factor which gives an indication of the influence which the wind has on the temperature and hence comfort. Ignoring this chill factor gives a false impression. As the wind increases in velocity so does its cooling effect (see Table 2).

With some buildings, heat loss in winter can be considerable at times of strong winds due to increased convection of the heat that has passed through the structure and envelope of the building as well as the increased infiltration of the colder air from outside. For the most part, this infiltration should be controlled by construction detailing, however at entrance doors special provision should be made to ensure that this infiltration is kept to a minimum by providing draught lobbies with two sets of draught-proofed doors sufficiently far apart to ensure that one door is closed before the other is opened. Where traffic is very heavy, such as in doors to shops or railway stations, other precautions may have to be taken (for example, a warm air curtain or revolving door which is particularly effective against cold air infiltration).

Where cold winter winds are common the careful siting of buildings and the location of wind breaks and shelter belts can have considerable effect on the heating load of buildings. The closer the

Table 2   Cooling effect of wind.

Windspeed km/h		Perceived temperature when real temp is 10° C
0	calm	10° C
5	light air	8° C
20	gentle breeze	2° C
40	strong breeze	−2° C

building is to the shelter belt the greater will be the reduction in heating load. Buildings also act as obstructions to wind, creating highly protected areas immediately behind but also creating turbulence further away unless they are specifically designed to provide deflection or guidance. In most cases designers will be coping with a site with existing buildings in the vicinity and the influence of these on the direction and velocity of wind, and hence on the heating load, on the new building must be considered. Tall slab buildings can produce wind speeds in their immediate vicinity of up to twice that which would occur if the building was not there. Tall buildings raised on columns and providing an open space underneath can produce a wind speed under the building of up to three times that which would exist in the absence of that building. Where these tall buildings are isolated the increased wind speeds affect an area approximately equal to the height of the building but with groups of tall buildings the calculation of wind speed is much more complex.

In addition to the problems of heating load on buildings caused by wind the designer must also consider the effect that wind will have on the use of outside spaces around the building and also on the cooling effects of summer breezes.

From Table 2 it will be readily seen that with an air shade temperature of 22° C the wind can make the difference between whether one would wish to sit out or hurry indoors (with zero wind velocity the perceived temperature would be 22° C but with a 30 km/h velocity the perceived temperature would be only 12° C which is quite cool). Thus in cool temperate climates like Britain all outdoor areas that are to be used for passive activity need to be sheltered to some degree. The level of shelter will depend upon the activity, the part of the country in which the site is located and its altitude, and the age or other specific peculiarities of the people using that space. For example a children's playground, for say 5- to 12-year-olds, need not be sheltered to the same extent as an outdoor sitting area for elderly people who require a fully protected sun-trap.

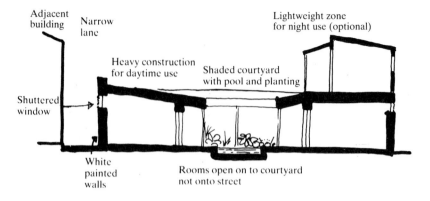

Figure 5   Design for hot-arid zone house.

As previously mentioned in the section on sun, designers in Britain have rarely concerned themselves with considerations of keeping buildings cool in summer. However, in warmer climates this is of particular importance. Broadly speaking, there are two types of warm/hot summer climatic zones, namely the hot–humid and the hot–arid, both of which require a totally different approach on the part of the designer. In the hot–humid zones the cool breezes that blow over water (usually the sea) should be used to keep the body cool and as such should be encouraged to pass through buildings whilst in the hot–arid parts of the world the winds in summer are usually warm to hot, having blown over land masses. These winds introduce warmer air (and often dust) into the buildings by infiltration and also warm the structure and envelope of the building by convection. For buildings in these hot–arid zones it is usually necessary to divide the space into day and night areas and to treat each independently. The day zone should be designed almost like that of a building for a cooler winter climate with well-insulated walls which will take a long time to heat up, small openings properly draught-proofed with few, if any, windows on the windward side of the building, adequate shelter belts (if possible) and draught lobbies; the night zone, on the other hand, must be designed to let the heat, which builds up during the day quickly, escape as soon as the sun goes down and with it the greatest heat source and, very often, the wind. Thus the night zone should have light, uninsulated walls and roof with a reasonable amount of openable windows. Nights are usually much cooler than days in hot–arid zones and especially so in winter when the heat build up of the day may be desirable and thus, as in so many design problems, a

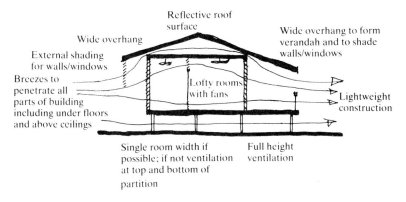

Figure 6   *Design for hot-humid zone house.*

compromise has to be reached which will depend upon whether summer heat or winter cold is the major consideration (see Figure 5).

In hot–humid zones the principal determinants are usually endeavouring to reduce the solar gain by buildings during the day whilst enabling cooling breezes to reach all parts of the interior during summer (and usually in spring and autumn as well) at the same time maximizing the solar gain in winter and providing protection against cool winter winds. Hot–humid zones usually receive most of their precipitation in the form of rain during the summer months and an added design consideration must be to enable the cooling breezes that accompany this rain (and which, in some parts, is the first relief from the oppressive heat) to penetrate to all parts of the building whilst the rain is falling. This calls for very wide overhangs over windows and other openings.

The point that the cooling breeze must be able to penetrate to all parts of the building has already been mentioned and as such it calls for conscious design decisions to be made. Figure 6 shows ways in which this can be achieved through full-height ventilation and cross ventilation. The use of fans can also be advantageous in keeping air moving throughout the interior. Plan arrangements should be as open as possible with large, lofty rooms being desirable to facilitate air movement.

In some parts of the world—especially the hotter parts, although not exclusively so—insects are a particular problem and buildings need to be protected from the penetration of these creatures. The usual method of excluding insects is the introduction of insect screening to all external doors and openable windows. The provision of insect screening cuts down on the velocity of breezes by acting as a filter and thus it may be necessary to consider increasing the amount of openable windows/shutters in such locations.

In many parts of the world buildings have to be designed to cope with the winds of very high velocities that occur during cyclones, typhoons or tornados. For the most part this is a structural problem involving careful choice of materials and proper detailing. However, the size and form of the building can contribute greatly to its effectiveness in combatting these problems (for example, the use of low-pitched roofs to reduce suction on the leeward slope of the building).

Precipitation

Precipitation in the form of rain and in some places, snow, has a considerable impact on the design of buildings. Most of the population of the developed world lives in areas that receive 250 mm of rain or more per year and therefore their buildings must be designed to protect the inhabitants from this. Not only does the quantity of precipitation per annum in a particular spot influence the design of the buildings but so does the form it takes and the frequency of its falling. Traditionally, this was reflected in the roof pitches and overhangs with steeper pitches being common in those parts of the world that experience snow or prolonged periods of light rain—such as northern Europe and Britain—whilst lower pitches are associated with warmer zones where snow is rare or unknown and where rain comes less frequently but usually at a much greater rate. Obviously roof pitches depend upon other factors such as the materials used for construction and covering but their traditional form was usually much more determined by climate than any other factor. Wide roof overhangs are required to throw rain and snow clear of the walls of buildings and thus to reduce the amount of moisture that reaches the wall surface whilst, as has been mentioned above under wind and sun, in hot–humid climates these broad overhangs are necessary to enable windows and doors to be kept open during heavy rainfall and to provide shading.

Precipitation affects the materials used to provide the external envelope of buildings in that where rainfall tends to be fairly light as in the south east of Britain (except along the actual coast), and other sheltered areas, it is traditional to clad buildings in a pervious material such as brick or stone of a minimum structural thickness, and which (by trial and error in the past) has proved to be such that before the moisture has penetrated to the inside of the building the rain will have stopped and the wall will dry out by evaporation aided by the sun and wind. Traditional buildings in areas of moderate or severe exposure have either had to employ very thick pervious masonry walls, adapt a form of cavity (as occurred in parts of Scotland long before cavity wall construction became common elsewhere in Britain) or use an impervious skin for the outside of the envelope —such materials include slate, tile, weatherboarding, and render. It is worth remembering that once a pervious material absorbs water its insulation value is reduced and thus heat is lost more rapidly from the interior. In Britain the Building Research Establishment has published *An Index of Exposure for Driving Rain* which combines wind and rain to show the variation over Britain of the severity of driving rain conditions.

The control of precipitation in building design is very much a part of the construction and detailing problem. It is essential that the design team appreciates the difficulties that arise with water penetration and the methods that should be employed to ensure that water does not enter the building or its structure under the most severe conditions that the building is likely to be subjected to in its locality. Invariably wind accompanies rain and this wind-blown rain must be taken into account in detailing. Rain can actually be blown in such a way that it is striking a part of a building in an upward direction and detailing must take this into account.

Apart from the extent of roof overhangs and other protection of windows and doors from rain, the use of pervious or impervious cladding materials and the size, number and distribution of rainwater goods on a building (all of which can have a major impact on the appearance of a building with the latter often being ignored at design stage), the design team must take into account the needs of the occupier or user when he enters or leaves the building when rain or snow is falling. At the very least the principal (ideally each) entrance to a building should have a canopy of adequate size outside it to enable people to raise or lower umbrellas before entering or venturing forth and/or to put down bags etc. whilst looking for keys or waiting to be admitted. On houses this shelter is especially important from a security angle as it enables householders to talk to casual callers on the doorstep during inclement weather without feeling under an obligation to invite them inside. In addition to this, access to motor and other transport vehicles should preferably be under cover wherever practical and, indeed this is an essential when designing for disabled persons (see Chapter 8). The carport is more practical in this respect than the traditional garage because even where there is covered access from the garage to the house it is very rare that it is possible to close the door on leaving in the car, or open same on returning, without getting wet although with remote control operated doors this is now possible, if expensive.

Where a number of buildings on a site are used by the same people requiring frequent access, covered ways should always be provided —these need not always be enclosed except in those parts of the world where the climate is particularly hostile or where access is required by special categories of people (for example, the elderly, very young children, or hospital patients).

Special provision may have to be made in buildings for storage of rainwear and for the drying of the same, whilst in countries where heavy snow is experienced provision has to be made in the design not only for the storage and drying of heavy outdoor wear but also for changing footwear and tidying up before entering the main part of the building. In addition, storage may be required for snow clearing gear, grit etc. near to entrances.

There is one further form of precipitation that needs mentioning, and that is hail. In temperate climates hail is not a great problem but in warmer climates hailstorms of great severity can be experienced which can cause great damage to roofs of buildings. In these parts of the world the choice of roof coverings will be influenced by this with a consequent effect on the appearance of the building.

Conclusion

A thorough understanding of the climate of the locality in which a building is to be built together with the responses necessary to maximize the advantages and minimize the disadvantages of the resulting weather conditions is essential to ensure that the most comfortable environment is provided for the user. If this is done an added bonus of reducing energy consumption will inevitably follow where heating and/or cooling is necessary.

References

British Standards Institute DD67: 1980 Draft for Development *Basic Data for the Design of Buildings: Sunlight* (British Standards Institute: London, 1980).

British Standards Institute DD73: 1982 Draft for Development *Basic Data for the Design of Buildings: Daylight* (British Standards Institute: London, 1980).

Building Research Establishment Digest No. 23 *An Index of Exposure to Driving Rain* (Building Research Establishment: Ware, 1962).

Burberry, P. *Mitchell's Building Construction Environment and Services* (Batsford: London, 1978).

Chandler, T. J. *The Climate of the British Isles* (Hutchinson: London, 1976).

Cowan, H. J. (ed.) *Solar Energy Applications in the Design of Buildings* (Applied Science: New York, 1980).

Griffiths, J. F. *Applied Climatology: An Introduction* (The Open University Press: Milton Keynes, 1976).

Olgay, V. *Design with Climate* (Princeton University Press: Cambridge, Mass, 1973).

4

Site influences

Introduction

Buildings are intrinsically linked to the site that they occupy and in
most cases buildings are designed for a specific site (see Plates 9 and
10), the exceptions being most temporary structures and certain
standard designs, mainly in the housing, industrial and agricultural
fields; however, even these usually have to be adapted to suit specific
site conditions—not always with the happiest of results (see Figure
7).

   The site influences the design of buildings in a variety of ways not
least of all by its size and cost but also through its ground conditions,
aspect, prospect or outlook, topography and the host of existing and
adjoining features such as buildings, trees and planting, services (or
lack of them), and noise sources.

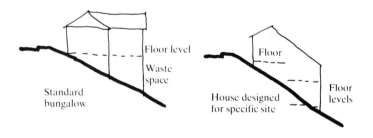

Figure 7   Building on a sloping site.

Plate 9   Robie House, Chicago, 1909 (Frank Lloyd Wright). Photo courtesy of: Julian Feary.

Size, shape, cost and ground conditions

Building sites vary enormously in size and cost and the buildings that are to be erected thereon will be influenced by these factors to a considerable extent. Even where a site is already owned by the client the value of the land will be able to be assessed together with its potential alternative uses. Land is usually scarce where buildings are needed, even in countries such as Australia and Canada (where most buildings are required in or near existing centres of population in the same way as in the densely populated countries of Europe). As land becomes scarcer the cost of such land rises and the demand for its more effective use results in increased densities and taller buildings, which inevitably influences the design of the buildings. Cost and size of plot are thus inevitably inter-related and it is commonplace to find that in most centres of population spacious, low-rise buildings are demolished and replaced with buildings of greater bulk producing more square metres of floor space per square metre of site. These bulkier buildings are more challenging to the design team and call for

47

every skill to be adopted. The planning process inevitably results in compromises having to be made (see Chapter 6) and this is never more likely than where the site size is small in relation to the size of the building required.

There are no hard and fast rules on ratio between building size and site size although local authorities often impose apparently arbitrary plot ratios i.e., the ratio between maximum floor space of the building and site area often with an allowance for roads, lanes or walkways along the boundaries of a site). For example a plot ratio of 2:1 would enable a site size of 1,000 m² to be developed with 2,000 m² of floor space. If the same site had a frontage of 50 m along a roadway of 12 m width and the local authority permitted 50 per cent of the roadway to be included in the 'site size' for plot ratio calculation this would increase the 'site size' by 50 m × 6 m or 30 m² to 1,030 m² enabling 2,060 m² of floor space. This can be a very valuable concession especially in the case of a corner site.

Other restrictions may be imposed by authorities such as a maximum site cover of (say) 50 per cent, the preservation of an existing building line, or the maintenance of certain minimum distances from site boundaries either for reasons of preventing fire spread, access, angles of light or to prevent overlooking. All of these have the effect of restricting the area of the site upon which building can take place.

Within these parameters there are often many solutions. For example, the problem of a site of 10,000 m² upon which a building containing 10,000 m² of floor space is required can be solved by building a single-storey building of 10,000 m² covering the whole site (unless other restrictions mentioned above apply) or a two-storey building of 50,000 m² per floor plus vertical access or even a ten-storey building of 1,000 m² per floor plus vertical access (see Figure 8). It will be up to the design team, bearing in mind all the other design requirements, to decide which permutation is the most appropriate.

Cramped sites can have an effect on the type of structure chosen for the building. Certain structural forms, such as steel frames may have to be eliminated from the alternatives to be considered because of the lack of space for actual erection.

The shape of the site will, unless the site is very spacious, influence the shape of the building and can often pose further problems for the design team. Long, thin, rectangular sites pose different problems to

Plate 10 (facing)   Falling Water, Bear Run, Pennsylvania, 1936 (Frank Lloyd Wright). Photo courtesy of: ARCAID.

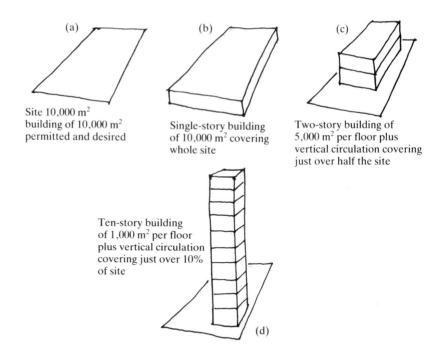

Site 10,000 m²
building of 10,000 m²
permitted and desired

Single-story building
of 10,000 m² covering
whole site

Two-story building of
5,000 m² per floor plus
vertical circulation covering
just over half the site

Ten-story building
of 1,000 m² per floor
plus vertical circulation
covering just over 10%
of site

Figure 8   Alternative solutions providing the same useable floor space on the same site: (a) site; (b) solution 1; (c) solution 2; (d) solution 3.

square sites or irregular sites. Figure 9 shows three solutions to the same building problem. In Figure 9(a) the building plan reflects the shape of the site and presents a narrow frontage to the street with long side walls which could present problems of overlooking and lack of privacy over and from adjacent sites. In Figure 9(b) the building runs across the site presenting a wide frontage to the street and short side walls which would inevitably have to be blank as they are shown built up to the boundary. This could still result in lack of privacy from the street but full privacy is maintained to the rear (depending upon position of adjacent buildings). However, unless some tunnel access can be provided at ground level there will be no direct way through to the rear of the site. In Figure 9(c) a square building is provided giving side access and ideally few windows other than those for service rooms on the sides—privacy is virtually as good as in Figure 9(b).

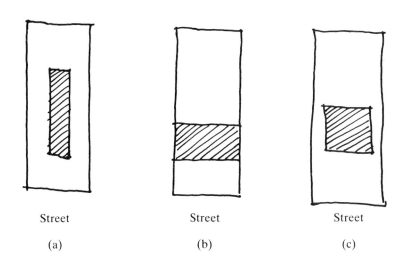

Street	Street	Street
(a)	(b)	(c)

Figure 9   Plans showing different solutions to positioning a building on a site.

Even on very spacious sites the decision on the location of the building can result in problems because of the constraints of size, shape and cost although such problems will usually be minor compared with those of cramped sites.

Where residential buildings are proposed, local authorities often impose densities relating to either persons, habitable rooms or houses to the hectare. These densities, especially when they are high (for example, over 300 persons per hectare), have the same effect as reducing site size and have often, in the past, resulted in high-rise flatted solutions. It is interesting to remember that it is possible to design housing at up to 300 persons per hectare where everyone has their own ground level entrance and even a small garden (see Figure 10).

The ground conditions on a particular site will affect the design of a building principally through the structural method chosen which will relate to the foundation type. Where a site is of poor load-bearing capacity a light-weight building will be necessary, which may mean that there is a restriction on the height of the building that could be constructed. If a raft foundation has to be used a simple square or rectangular plan will probably be essential. The ground water level can determine whether a building will have a basement or not.

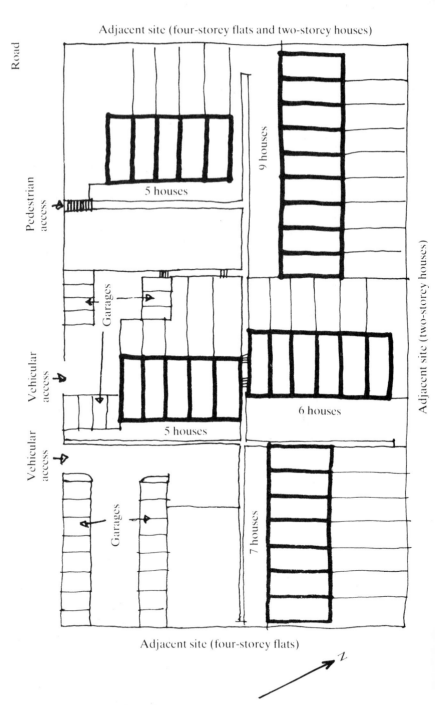

Figure 10 Site plan showing houses in urban fabric built to a high density, all with front door at ground level, gardens and off-street parking. (Based on a design by Andrews, Sherlock and Partners, architects, London.)

Aspect

Desirable aspects for rooms and spaces within buildings vary with the climate of the locality and even the microclimate of the site. As has been discussed in Chapter 3 good architecture reflects the climate of the area and in the planning of buildings the most effective use of the prevailing climate should be made. It is not possible to change the climate but it is possible to design our buildings to modify it to our advantage. Buildings should be positioned on site and planned in such a way that all rooms and spaces take the fullest advantage of desirable climatic features whilst excluding, as far as possible, the less desirable. In colder climates this usually means maximizing sun penetration and minimizing the effects of cold winds on entrances and outdoor areas (see Chapter 3).

Prospect and daylight

Since the advent of transparent glass the outlook from rooms and spaces within buildings has taken on increasing importance. One of the great principles of the modern movement was maximizing the use of glass to enable the interior of buildings to appear to flow from the exterior.

Whether we are involved with buildings for living or for working in a pleasant outlook is desirable whilst some daylight and sunlight are essential for health (see Chapter 3). Certain buildings, such as shops, theatres and factories may not be able to have an outward look in the same way as residential, office, and educational buildings but these exceptions are few and they have their own internal prospect—bustling shoppers, stage performance, or dynamic industrial processes.

In the 1960s it was fashionable in some circles to talk of 'windowless' buildings, the principle being that the controlled internal environment of air conditioning and artificial lighting could produce a more constant working space. Fortunately few of these buildings were built and whilst physical bodily comfort was perhaps better, psychologically the buildings were not popular as people like to be able to be at least aware of what is going on outside and to see what the weather is like.

The amount of daylight required inside any building is dependent upon the nature of the activity being performed in that space as well as the reflection within that space from walls, floors, ceilings, and furniture. The desired dependence upon and efficiency of artificial light must also be considered. The amount of daylight reaching a

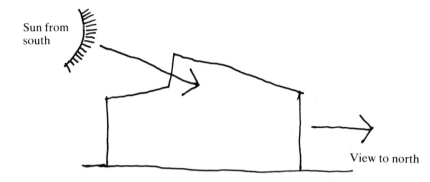

Sun from
south

View to north

*Figure 11   Section through room showing how view and sun
penetration can be achieved (northern hemisphere example).*

particular surface from a window, skylight or other opening needs
careful consideration in relation to the layout of a building's interior.
This can be calculated using daylight protractors or Waldram
diagrams.

Buildings must be designed in such a way that they maximize
natural lighting. This means that wherever possible rooms should be
located on outside walls and should not be too deep in plan. On top
floors, or in single-storey buildings daylight can be provided by
clerestory windows or rooflights, whilst the careful use of courtyards
and atruims can permit natural lighting to enter rooms and spaces
that would, otherwise, have to rely on artificial lighting. In order to
maximize daylight penetration glazed areas need to extend as high as
possible within rooms.

If a building site enjoys a fine view (either from ground level or from
upper floors if these are proposed) this should be exploited to the full.
Rooms where people will spend a lot of time, especially residential
living rooms, should be located to take advantage of this view. In
domestic buildings this may mean putting living rooms on the first
floor with bedrooms on the ground in order to maximize a view.
Rarely will view and ideal aspect coincide and often a compromise
must be reached. The use of 'through' rooms or clerestory lighting can
often overcome this conflict (see Figure 11). One major advantage of
northern views in the northern hemisphere and southern views in the
southern hemisphere is that the view is lit by the sun and thus there is
a greater play of sun and shadow than where the view is into the sun
(see Figures 12 and 13).

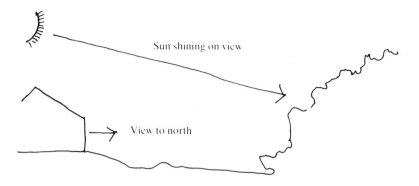

Figure 12   Sunlit view (northern hemisphere).

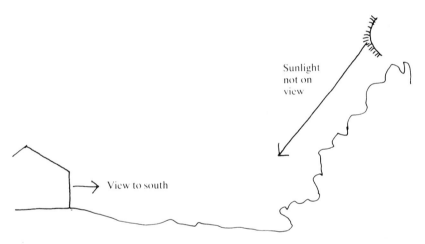

Figure 13   Shaded view (northern hemisphere).

A fine prospect need not, of course, be natural or distant. It may be a well-landscaped garden or courtyard, some other buildings or bustling activity. The latter is very important for elderly people or hospital patients, many of whom soon get bored with a fine view over fields or a similar fairly static outlook—the fact that the view may change only a few times a year (or less) may further emphasize time to them. If the outlook is over a busy road, a bustling pedestrian area, a park or other activity area and provided there is security from invasion and insulation from noise, elderly people will be far happier (see Figure 14).

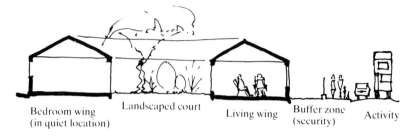

Figure 14   Section through old people's home.

   If buildings are designed to maximize views it is vital that people using the spaces can see the views from their normal position —window sills must be low enough for people in beds, armchairs or office chairs (or whatever they will use within the space) to be able to see out (see Figures 15 and 16). One of the tragedies of high-rise living is that residents so often cannot see the view from a seated position (see Figure 17); all they can see is sky and unbroken sky whether it is blue or grey is boring.

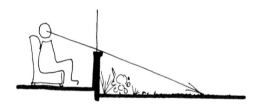

Figure 15   Views can be appreciated: (a) in a ground-floor example; (b) in an upper-floor example.

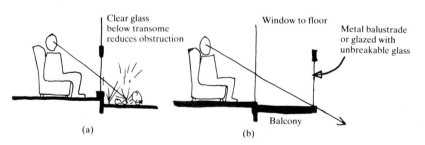

Figure 16   Low-rise or ground-floor sill obstructs much of a view if over 600 mm or if the ground slopes away from the building.

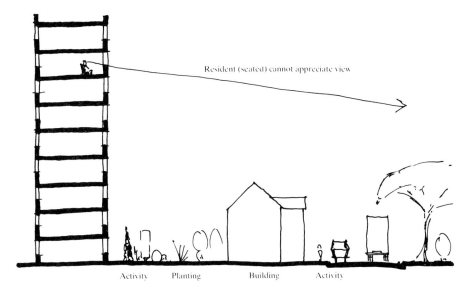

Figure 17   High-rise block.

Topography

One of the major differences between the way the Ancient Greeks and the Ancient Romans designed their buildings was that the Greeks blended their buildings into the site whilst the Romans levelled their sites first. The Acropolis in Athens is probably one of the finest groups of buildings in the world and here the buildings maximize their hilltop position by exploiting the changes in level and slopes to the full—the Erectheion is perhaps the best example of this. By contrast the Colloseum in Rome sits on a flat site carved out of a hillside.

Closer to our own time Frank Lloyd Wright (see Chapter 1) showed in his domestic buildings how a building should respect the topography of the site. His Prairie houses of the 1890s and 1900s on the almost totally flat Illinois countryside near Chicago are very different from his famous Falling Water, Bear Run, Pennsylvania where the ground slope, rock structure and waterfall have been fully exploited (see Plates 9 and 10).

Very few building sites are totally flat but most buildings require level floors and whilst we have come to accept changes in levels as we

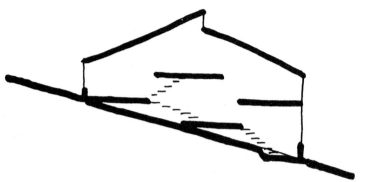

Figure 18   Section through building that maximizes sloping site by change of level.

approach buildings (often ceremonial) and several floors within buildings all requiring vertical transportation (stairs, lifts, or escalators) the maximizing of slopes by changing levels within buildings is less common (see Figure 18).

Providing one does not change level at inconvenient places (for example between the kitchen and the dining room) and providing provision is made for elderly and disabled persons, these changes of level can result in very interesting internal spaces whilst externally the building will blend in with its surroundings much better. Speculative builders have often produced interesting terraces of houses climbing hillsides (such as those in Bath, Edinburgh and Sydney, see Plate 11) although it was rare for the ground slope to be maximized within individual dwellings. This is because wherever possible, on sloping sites, narrow buildings should be built along the contour lines in order to minimize excavation and/or complex structures. However, sloping sites do invariably result in fine views, and changes in level within the buildings can often maximize the benefit from these views.

Nevertheless, some building types demand flat sites (for example industrial buildings where large areas of unbroken floor space are essential for production) but for the most part gently sloping sites are best for building due to the natural draining characteristics of such sites.

Existing and adjoining features

Few buildings are built on totally virgin sites in splendid isolation and even in these cases natural features invariably exist. The principal

Plate 11   *Late nineteenth-century speculative housing on a hillside in Sydney, New South Wales. Photo courtesy of: New South Wales Government.*

features affecting building design are often existing buildings, natural features such as trees, planting and areas of water, noise sources, and services (or the lack of same).

Existing buildings

Existing buildings will have considerable bearing upon the design of adjacent buildings. In some places, especially on infil sites where buildings occupy the whole of the site and where the new facade is flush or almost flush with adjacent facades, limitations upon the design of the new facade may be imposed by the local authorities who may require 'matching up' to be done to such an extent that a facsimile reproduction of adjacent buildings is the only answer. In other cases limitations on use of materials and proportions that match may be required and even where no such restrictions apply the design team will wish to apply good manners to its design (see also Chapter 7).

On less confined sites adjacent buildings can impose constraints other than aesthetic in that they may cast shadows over the site or provide uncomfortable wind movements—windows may overlook (see Figure 19) or the existing building may produce some form of environmental pollution such as noise or fumes from industrial or other processes (see Figure 20) which must be taken account of in the design of the building. It may well be the new building that produces these problems for adjacent existing buildings and it is thus vital that the design team alleviate these. In many cases the planning authority's requirements will prevent the worst excesses but rarely does it address itself to problems of micro-climatic impact (see Figure 21).

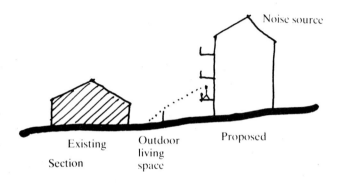

Figure 19   Destruction of privacy.

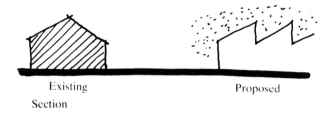

Figure 20   Noise pollution.

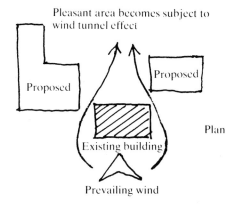

Figure 21   Microclimatic impact.

Services

It is rare that availability of services poses any constraints on the design of buildings in developed countries; in fact it is rather the converse. Where a main sewer runs across a site one is not usually permitted to build over it and a scheme may have to be adopted to cope with this problem where the additional costs of diverting the sewer are not warranted (see Figure 22).

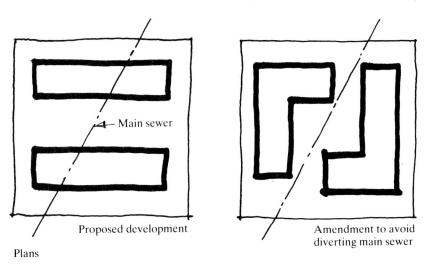

Figure 22   Main sewer on site can affect building development.

Plate 12   Eugowra Farmhouse, New South Wales, 1980 (John Andrews). Photo courtesy of: John Andrews International Pty Ltd, photographer David Moore.

On the other hand, the absence of services can have considerable impact on design—where piped gas is unavailable, as in many rural locations, provisions for the storage and replacement of gas cylinders, oil or solid fuel will have to be considered, and Plate 12 shows how the lack of mains water was turned into a positive design attribute on John Andrew's Eugowra farmhouse. The current energy crisis has turned people's attention to alternative sources of cheap, renewable energy such as solar and wind power and the impact of these on buildings can be considerable unless specifically designed for at conception stage (see Plate 8 and Figure 4). Even such services as vehicular access and rubbish collection can have an impact on design especially in housing developments.

Natural features

Few natural elements can enhance a building as much as trees. However, their impact on the design can be considerable. Problems of roots and moisture demand can affect foundations and drains and many people and authorities have a phobia extending almost to a paranoia about anything that grows more than about 1 m above the ground. Except for a few particularly moisture hungry trees (willows and poplars) buildings and trees can accommodate one another provided care is exercized at design, construction and subsequent maintenance stages. In some places, trees may have preservation orders or similar placed upon them and it is always wise to check whether this is the case before commencing a design on sites containing trees. Even where no such statutory protection exists everything should be done by the design team to protect mature trees.

It is important always to consider trees in their mature state—the 2 m high sapling can soon become 10 m or more in height with all the consequent problems unless this is borne in mind at design stage. In addition, clear distinction must be made between evergreen and deciduous trees. Evergreens will provide shade all year round and in many cases, even in warmer climates, this may not be desirable. In colder climates evergreens also restrict light during the winter months. Deciduous trees, fortunately, tend to follow the 'temperature cycle' rather than the 'daylight cycle' (see Chapter 3), and thus are usually still bare, or at least not fully foliated, in late spring when shade is not necessarily required whilst in late summer/early autumn—when temperatures are usually higher and shade is often welcome—these trees are fully foliated. Deciduous trees are especially useful in warmer climates to shade Eastern and Western facades. Trees can also be valuable in providing shelter belts to protect buildings against strong winds.

Good planting around buildings invariably improves the appearance of buildings providing softer shapes and more varied colours than can usually be obtained by other means—even window boxes can liven up an otherwise dull, harsh facade. Landscape architects should be involved in the design of projects from the very beginning, taking on an active role as a member of the design team. Landscaping should form an integral part of the design and not be treated as an afterthought. Allowing the provisional sum of £x for planting is a recipe for cutting this item out as costs escalate during the building stage as they invariably do. It is also important that the correct plants be incorporated and where existing plants or landscaped areas exist they should be considered from the beginning (see Figure 23). Planting can also be used to absorb traffic noise and fumes.

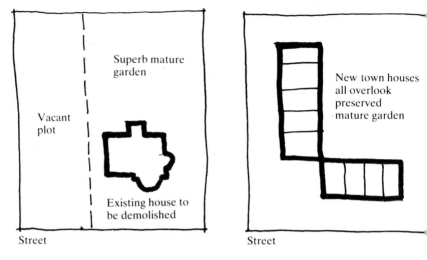

Figure 23   New houses maximizing existing mature garden.

Bodies of water such as streams, rivers, lakes or the sea can affect a building's design and where these occur they should be exploited to the full (see Plate 10). Care must be exercized where bodies of water exist in close proximity to buildings because of the effect of moisture and salt on the buildings' fabric and environment. Large bodies of water can result in mists and possibly also in flooding. The ground water level is usually relatively high in these cases and this can affect the type of foundation chosen, which in turn could affect the type of structure selected for the building.

Noise sources (see also Chapter 5)

When the history books about the late twentieth century are written, the scourge of noise will probably feature in the same way as the appalling sanitation of the early nineteenth century colours our thoughts on that period. Traffic, trains, aircraft, transistor radios, neighbours' stereos, and television as well as industrial noise all add to the more natural noises of children playing, animals, wind etc. and often totally drown these.

Where buildings have to be built near major noise sources special precautions must be taken to protect the inhabitants from the noise. These can vary from double glazing and air-conditioning, which is expensive in both initial and running costs, to turning the building's back on the noise. Where the noise source is easily determined and from one direction this is relatively simple and several examples of blocks of flats backing on to motorways and railways have been built (see Plates 13 and 14) whilst in Newcastle upon Tyne the Byker Wall flats turn their back on a motorway which was never (and is now unlikely to be) built. Simpler solutions incorporating banking and planting can be adopted where traffic is less but is nevertheless an irritant.

Aircraft noise is a more difficult problem to solve with roofs of 'heavy mass' construction, double glazing and air conditioning being the only total solution. This is essential for buildings within close proximity to airports. Fortunately recent designs of aircraft are quieter and whilst this problem will not go away it is becoming more bearable.

Reproduced noise (radio, television, and stereo) is a further problem. Within buildings, construction techniques and finishings are available to reduce the transmission or absorb same (see Chapter 5) and this combined with the physical separation through zoning (see Chapter 6) can contribute extensively. However, noise can be transmitted from buildings to the outside and hence into other buildings which can be a particular problem where high-density living occurs

Plate 13   Housing, Shepherds' Bush, Greater London, 1983 (Pollard Thomas Edwards & Associates).

Plate 14   Housing, Shepherds' Bush, Greater London, 1983 (Pollard Thomas Edwards & Associates). Photo courtesy of: Pollard, Thomas Edwards and Associates, photographer Horst Kolo.

accentuated even more in warmer climates (and on warm days in cooler climates) when windows and doors are open. Planting, banking, and noise baffles can all help but apart from others turning their volumes down or incorporating 'white (or masking) noise' little can be done to alleviate the problem completely (see Figure 24).

Conclusion

A careful analysis of the constraints imposed and potential offered by the site is essential at the Design Stage to ensure that the proposed building will become an intrinsic part of the site exploiting its attributes and offering a sound solution to its drawbacks.

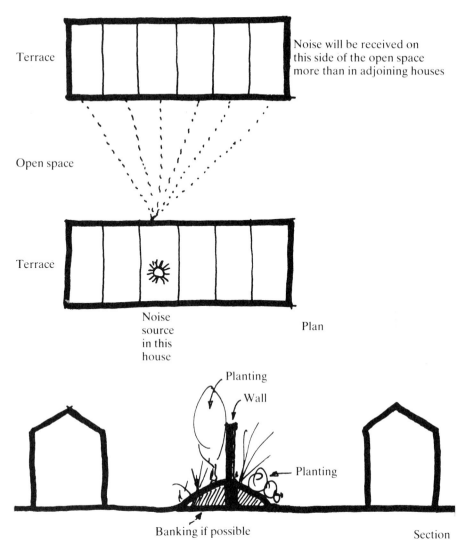

Figure 24   Problems of noise emissions in parallel terraces showing possible method of reducing this problem.

References

Aldous T. (ed.) *Trees and Buildings: Complement or Conflict* (RIBA: London, 1979).

British Standards Institute DD73: 1982 Draft for Development *Basic Data for the Design of Buildings: Daylight* (BSI: London, 1982).

British Standards Institute CP 3: Chapter 111 1972 *Sound Insulation and Noise Reduction* (BSI: London, 1972).

Judd, S. and Dean, J. (eds) *Medium Density Housing in Australia* (RAIA, 1983).

67

5

Technological, economic and legal influences

Introduction

The impact on the design of buildings of technological, economic, and legal constraints has increased rapidly since the Industrial Revolution. Nowadays these constraints can often determine whether a building will be built or not. Too often the results of these constraints can result in a building that does not give the element of delight we mentioned previously and which is expanded upon in Chapter 7. This need not be the case. Perhaps it is better in this chapter to think in terms of these influences being challenges rather than constraints.

Influence of materials

On traditional buildings the availability of materials was of paramount importance to the design. Local materials were used at all times for modest—and for the bulk of more important—buildings. The use of materials that could not be won or processed in the close vicinity of the building was restricted by difficulties of transportation. Until the advent of the railways, most building materials that had to be transported any distance had to be moved by water, as roads in most parts of the world were not of a particularly high standard. Even when the railways were in fairly common use throughout Britain in the latter part of the nineteenth century there could often be difficulty with transporting building materials from railheads as the cost of such transport grew considerably as the distance from the goods depot increased. This, however, changed with the advent of the motor lorry which came into its own during World War I.

These local venacular materials gave buildings a character all of their own and the designers (in the broadest sense) had to adapt their buildings to suit the particular materials. For example, the pitch of the roof was controlled by the precipitation in the area and also by the roof covering that was generally available (see Chapter 3). In those parts of the country where flint was the only available material, buildings tended to have rounded corners and very low walls. The availability and use of hardwoods for framing of timber buildings shows quite marked differences in the north west of England from that found in East Anglia and the south east. This was due principally to the fact that much better quality timber was still available in the north west at a much later date than in the south east where relatively young timbers had to be used for most work.

The Industrial Revolution not only enabled a much better transport system to be developed, but it also resulted in an increase in the number of manufactured materials, which thus became available to building designers. Materials such as iron and glass had been available for hundreds of years. However, the better production techniques that became available during the nineteenth century enabled these materials to be used in buildings in a way hitherto never experienced. It also meant that these materials became much cheaper. With the advent of steel manufacture framed buildings became a possibility and we will see the impact of this later in this chapter. The nineteenth century saw the introduction of machine-made clay roof tiles which permitted a lower pitch than the hand-made variety whilst the advent of the railways enabled slates to be moved economically from Wales and other slate producing parts of the country to the growing urban areas in the midlands, the south and the north west. The economical clay brick, which hitherto had been confined to those parts of the country where no good building stones existed, could now be transported by rail to many parts of the country and especially to these industrial centres. Another cheap nineteenth-century material which was not to find a vast use in Britain but was to prove a very economical material to transport by sea was corrugated sheet steel. This was to form the principal roof covering, and often wall cladding material, of many buildings built in those parts of the world that were then settled by the British—in particular Australia and New Zealand.

As the nineteenth century turned to the twentieth century many new manufactured materials were introduced which were to become of great value to the design team. Although concrete, in various forms, had been available since Roman times, it was not until the latter part of the nineteenth century that its potential as a material for building came to the forefront with the introduction of reinforcement (the controlled manufacture of Portland cement having been avail-

able earlier in the nineteenth century). New processes for the manufacture of glass enabled ever larger sheets to become available. This,
together with developments in plastics, aluminium, and other sheet
metals, as well as lightweight insulation materials have given the
design team much greater freedom than has ever been available to
them in the past. This freedom has not always been entirely successful, as many new materials and techniques have not withstood the
test of time nor have they always proved to be successful as far as
acceptance by the general public is concerned.

One of the major consequences of the change from indigenous
materials to manufactured materials has meant that buildings can be
built to look very much the same in any part of the world, as raw
materials are shipped from one country to another and similar
manufacturing processes are set up not only in the older industrial
countries but also in newly developing ones. In selecting a material it
is not only necessary to consider its present availability but it is also
desirable to take into account the possibility or otherwise of being
able to obtain a suitable replacement if the material is damaged in any
way during its life. Substitute materials are not always successful
either from the point of view of aesthetics, nor of compatability with
the older material. Thus when the design team selects materials for
the building it will be involved in making decisions that will have far
reaching effects on the design of the building.

It is particularly necessary to consider the structural integrity of a
building material, how it will behave if exposed to fire, as far as
breakdown of the material is concerned, the spread of flame along the
surface of the material and also whether any toxic gases would be
given off by the material in the unfortunate event of a fire.

The way that a material will weather must also be carefully
considered. Some materials such as glass are affected very little by
weather and in fact undergo virtually no change over many years of
exposure to the elements. Other materials undergo quite an abrupt
change very quickly when exposed to the elements (for example,
copper which oxidizes and changes from its original copper colour to
green in a very short period). The exposure of many materials to the
weather will result in their undergoing a slow but definite change;
sometimes their colour will change slightly over the years, in other
cases the surface may well erode (as can happen with some stones) or
the material may break down altogether (as would be the case with
most timbers if they are not suitably treated with paint or other
preservatives). The design team must carefully consider these points.
In some cases they may want their building components to show
evidence of weathering, perhaps even earlier than would have nor-

mally been the case. An example of this may be an extension or alteration to an existing building which has weathered over many years, and in some cases advanced weathering techniques have been adapted. Not only must the weathering agents of wind, rain, and sun be considered on the materials but also the effects of such things as salt, windblown sand, industrial pollution, and high humidity.

The compatability of one material with another must be taken into account chemically where a reaction between one material and another can take place to the detriment of one or both the materials. Chemical action can occur as a result of water running over one material becoming slightly acidic and then passing over another material causing the latter material to corrode. In addition, compatibility of materials must also be considered physically as virtually all materials have different differential movements, some materials expanding and contracting, others such as concrete tending to creep; all these factors must be taken into account in the selection of materials.

The aesthetic value of materials must not be underestimated. The choice of materials will contribute greatly to the pattern, the texture and the colour of the different parts of a building surface (see Chapter 7). Some materials may have to be chosen because of their insulation properties, either from a thermal or an acoustic point of view whilst others will have to be specially selected to resist wear and tear (see Chapter 9).

Choice of structural form

There are two basic methods of producing a building, the first is where the walls and partitions become loadbearing elements carrying the weight of floors and roofs down to the foundations, whilst the second type involves the use of a framework of timber, steel or concrete which transmits loads by means of beams to columns which in turn transmit the loads to the ground. A third method of construction can also be considered, that of the tensile structure. However, these are more commonly associated with engineering works. Nevertheless a number of tensile building structures have been constructed, where a pylon or group of pylons have cables suspended from them. These in turn carry the structure of the building by suspension.

Loadbearing construction was normally the traditional method used and it is principally associated with brick or stone buildings with timber being the predominant material for floor and roof construction. Loadbearing walls are of particular value in buildings where a continuous form of enclosure is required and also where the interior needs to be divided in a fairly regular pattern to form smaller rooms or spaces and where these smaller rooms and spaces are repeated on upper floors. It is possible to transmit loads via the walls and partitions and in effect to combine the load-bearing and separation functions of the walls and partitions. By the time a brick wall for a two- to three-storey building is built thick enough to withstand the elements and provide a reasonable degree of thermal insulation, it is also thick enough to carry the superimposed loads of floors and roofs and to provide the necessary sound insulation. It follows that for low-rise buildings requiring a number of different rooms such as domestic buildings, loadbearing walls and partitions will often prove to be the most economical both in relation to cost and to the space occupied by them. One drawback with loadbearing construction is that it is much less adaptable than framed construction and it is therefore more difficult, if not impossible, to remove walls and partitions. As a result the rearrangement of spaces is not particularly easy (see Chapter 6).

For buildings over four storeys in height or where large internal spaces or a flexible layout is required, or where large open spaces are needed on the ground and/or on the first floors, with small spaces above, for example in a hotel, then a framed building will probably prove to be the most desirable choice. Framed buildings are not new (many Tudor buildings involved a frame) and traditional box frame and cruck construction which can be found in different parts of England fully exploit the frame principle. By the end of the medieval period the perpendicular style of church architecture was such that effectively it was a framed building. The stone ribs of the vaulting being gathered on stone columns transmitted their load straight down to the foundations, whilst the spaces between these columns were filled with an intricate pattern of glass and thin stone. Nowadays, frames for buildings are usually constructed in steel or concrete. Without the steel frame it would have been impossible to have built buildings as tall as are currently being constructed. The first building to maximize the potential of the steel frame for multi-storey work was Louis Sullivan's Guaranty Life Building in Buffalo, New York. Had a loadbearing form of construction been chosen for this particular example the amount of floor space needed on the lower floors to provide the loadbearing capacity would have been such that these valuable rentable spaces would have been completely lost and the building would have been uneconomical. Frame construction is of great use for single-storey buildings covering large areas such as industrial and exhibition buildings. These have their roots in the earliest industrial buildings such as Crystal Palace and the great train sheds of the middle to late nineteenth century.

The use of a framed building invariably means the acceptance of some form of grid or pattern of beams and columns which will immediately impose certain constraints upon the design team. The structural engineer would normally advise whether a steel or concrete frame would be the most appropriate depending on such factors as site, location, bearing capacity of ground, shape, size, number of storeys and height of building, fire resistance requirements, maximum size of clear floor area required, construction type, and economics. In conjunction with the quantity surveyor and the architect, the structural engineer will also recommend the most appropriate grid size and other construction such as upper floors and roof. For single-storey industrial type buildings the steel frame is usually found to be the most economical, whilst in most parts of the world for multi-storey buildings the concrete frame proves the better buy in the majority of cases.

Whilst the selected grid invariably poses constraints on the design team the use of a frame building opens up much greater avenues of freedom in layout and in choice of methods of enclosure. Without the necessity to carry loads the other functional requirements of the walls and partitions can be exploited to the full. It is possible to maximise the potential of the external envelope for admitting natural light by means of incorporating large expanses of glass, although the poor thermal and acoustic insulation properties of glass must be taken into account at this time. Other materials can be used to provide an opaque envelope with a high degree of fire resistance, thermal and sound insulation which in turn will occupy a very small amount of valuable floor space. The perimeter of the frame can be exposed or concealed either in brick or stone or by means of a curtain wall. Internally spaces can be divided either by permanent non-loadbearing partitioning, removable partitioning or temporary partitioning in order to satisfy such requirements as sound and thermal insulation, fire separation, privacy, exclusion of unwanted smells, and spacial desirability of providing either large wide-open spaces or smaller intimate spaces.

The incorporation of services is often easier in framed buildings than in those of loadbearing construction and special provision can be made much more easily for them. In order to maximize the potential flexibility of framed buildings, services must be designed with this in mind. This applies especially to heating and cooling services.

Space and tensile structures have traditionally been associated with temporary structures such as the tent or alternatively with engineering works such as bridges. They are, however, useful where large uncluttered floor areas are required such as in aircraft hangars or where it is essential to avoid columns along one side such as for example in a stadium. The form produced by such tensile structures is usually such a unique and dominating element of the design that it is essential for the design team to work in very close collaboration to ensure that maximum value can be gained from adopting this type of structure.

Services

One of the principal constraints applicable to buildings nowadays is that imposed by services. Whilst the design team should not allow the requirements of services to dictate layout or appearance it must, nevertheless, ensure that these are incorporated in an economical, efficient and easy to maintain way. Services take up space and adequate space must always be provided to ensure the most efficient services system (see also Chapter 6).

The earliest 'service' as such included in buildings was the fire to provide heat, light, and cooking facilities. Gradually the introduction of water supply and water-borne sewerage systems together with more sophisticated forms of heating changed the form and shape of buildings. By the early twentieth century the foundations of modern services had been laid with the advent of gas, telephone, and electricity together with lifts, electrical pumps, mechanical ventilation, central heating, and air conditioning. These allowed taller and deeper buildings to be developed with large open spaces. It has been during the last couple of decades, however, that developments in the services sphere of great significance have occurred. The computer has enabled more sophisticated controls to be applied to service installation and itself has demanded new solutions to building design to enable its potential use to be maximized. Many office buildings built in the 1950s and 1960s are difficult if not impossible to convert to accommodate the information technology which the computer, together with cable television and other continuing developments have given us.

The energy crisis of 1973 has resulted in design teams taking a much closer look at their building designs in order to minimize energy consumption. In Chapter 3 we looked at ways in which the best features of the climate of any locality can be maximized to produce energy—efficient building. In the economics section of this chapter (see pp. 77–84) we look at alternative solutions for minimizing energy consumption.

Wherever possible water-borne services should be grouped together with the services themselves running in straight lines and being easily accessible for maintenance purposes. In buildings over one storey in height, rooms with services should be placed above one another and any hot or cold water tanks should be located as close as possible to the outlets or at least to the outlets most frequently used.

Services wear out more quickly than any other building component and can start to need replacement after as little as ten years. A good design will provide for this by allowing adequate space and accessibility to enable this work to be carried out. On the Centre Beaubourg, Paris, (see Plate 15) the services are placed externally for this very reason.

Acoustic and noise performance

Noise has been defined as unwanted sound. It is important, therefore, in the design of buildings that all unwanted sound is excluded. In the past it has generally been a case of remedying previous omissions on

Plate 15   Centre Beaubourg, Paris, 1977 (Rogers & Piano). Photo courtesy of: Architectural Press.

the part of the design team to exclude sound. At the design stage it is necessary to anticipate and control the noise by design. The general environment tends to be much noisier now than it was several decades ago. One writer who grew up in the 1920s in the country in England has said that he grew up in the last of the silent eras. In urban areas, sound comes from people, traffic, aircraft, machinery as well as in the form of reproduced sound from hi-fi equipment, television etc. Even in rural areas the noise of tractors, aeroplanes spraying crops, and so forth can drown out the sound of animals, birds and the wind rustling in the trees. Proper control of noise in buildings involves decisions at all stages from the choice of the site to the smallest detail such as a window seal. Noises that are acceptable in daytime are often very annoying at night.

There are two forms of sound that the design team must consider in building design—impact sound and airborne sound. The former comes principally from footsteps on floors and stairs and the banging of windows and doors; it requires careful choice of floor and stair construction and finishings and selection of the doors, and windows, and frames, together with such items as self-closing devices for doors. Airborne sound is more often a planning problem and this is discussed in Chapters 4 and 6.

Noise transmission between parts of the building must also be considered. One way of doing this is to mark up a set of drawings of the building with those areas where noise is likely to be produced and those areas where quiet is going to be desirable, or essential. This can lead to noise zoning (see Chapter 6). However, zoning is only part of the solution as the plan of a building is invariably a compromise between conflicting demands such as circulation, structure, costs, etc. 'Acoustic targets' should be set for each part of the scheme. These should cover such factors as background noise level, reverberation time, privacy, vibration sensibility, and impact noise control. The usual way for controlling noise emitted from very noisy rooms is to adopt very massive construction to help sound insulation. However, where noisy rooms are going to be located higher up in buildings it may be necessary to use separate construction rather than massive construction in order to reduce the load on the building, Plant is always a problem and can be very noisy in many buildings. It is important that the sound output of all mechanical and electrical plant is considered carefully at the selection stage. It may be easier and more economical to purchase a more expensive but quieter piece of plant than to purchase a noisier piece that requires much more complex sound insulation. Plant that is underpowered for its peak demand can also prove to be very noisy. With services, one of the most important factors for reducing sound is to ensure that there is plenty of space. If services are cramped noise is very likely to be the result.

In order to minimize the impact of noise the structure of the building needs to be taken into account. Outside walls and roofs should be designed to keep noise in or out, depending on where the main noise source is, and where it is decided to construct a separate structure, then early decisions need to be made, in particular with regard to such things as the effect on services and on cost. In some cases, space is also needed for sound-lock lobbies. Good detailing is obviously essential if sound is going to be prevented from passing from one part of a building to another, and in addition good site supervision is essential; a small hole around a pipe can cause considerable vibration. Ideally, of course, there should be a high degree of feedback. However, this is rarely the case as we have seen when we dealt with design process.

Economic

> For which of you, intending to build a tower,
> sitteth not down first, and counteth the cost,
> whether he have sufficient to finish it?
> Lest haply, after he hath laid the foundations,
> and is not able to finish it, all that behold it,
> begin to mock him,
> saying, this man began to build, and was not
> able to finish.
>
> *Luke 14 vs 28–30*

As in the apostle Luke's time, almost all buildings proposed today have to comply with a budget and the tightness or otherwise of this budget will depend upon many factors. Normally the principal one will be the availability of funds to the client and, in most cases, the return on capital invested. There are, of course, buildings provided on a social basis (usually funded by central or local government, for example schools and hospitals) which do not provide a return on investment in any tangible sense; here the technique of cost-benefit analysis can be used to ascertain the 'worth' of such buildings and also to compare the advantages in monetary terms of two essentially different projects.

One of the most common techniques that the design team will employ to ensure the best value for money in the building will be that known as cost planning. Cost planning is the process by which projects can be costed at the design stage in such a way that a clear statement of the various issues is provided showing the cost implications of the different courses of action open to the design team.

The design team will be concerned with considering various alternatives which can have an impact on cost. It will analyse the initial cost and the running costs and the different solutions for producing the same building at lower cost. It could also extend its role to considering whether a different building which would produce greater returns employing the same resources should be built instead.

Cost control in building is necessary not only to ensure that the total expenditure is kept within the amount agreed by the client in the early stages of the design process, but also to ensure that the client obtains good value for money and that the funds are distributed between the various parts of the building in a balanced and logical way. Good value for money means a well constructed, workable, and aesthetically pleasing building. The design team must look at the total cost of building projects and not be simply concerned with the initial capital cost. The running and maintenance costs of the building throughout its projected life or capital return period must be considered despite the difficulty of this exercise.

Some design solutions will prove cheaper to build and run than others but the cheapest solutions will not necessarily provide more user satisfaction than the more expensive designs—in fact, the converse is usually (but by no means universally) true. In general, it is the simpler design solutions that prove to be the most economic. If layouts, forms and shapes are kept simple, if the structure is straightforward and uncomplicated, if the range of materials and products employed is limited and if the services are kept to a minimum and laid out in a simple way the building should always prove to be more economic than if all these matters are complex. Nor should the design team assume that because it has produced a very simple solution to a problem that it will be less desirable than a more complex solution from an aesthetic point of view. However, there are few designers who have the ability to produce simple buildings that are also beautiful. Mies van der Rohe was one and his Barcelona Pavillion (see Plate 16) shows an extremely simple solution to the problem of designing a prestige but temporary exhibition building. The materials employed are of a very high quality and the detailing is superb. Few could argue that the beauty in this building is not to be found in its simplicity. Nevertheless, this simplicity of form, shape and detailing is not always easy to achieve and, in some cases, may prove more expensive to produce than apparently complex solutions.

Plate 16   Pavillion, Barcelona, 1929 (Mies van der Rohe). Photo courtesy of: British Architectural library RIBA.

Too often economics are allowed to become the prime determinant of buildings and the built results are all around us giving evidence of this. It is usually the design team who gets the blame when so often it has been the 'penny-pinching' requirements of the clients that have forced the design team's hand into producing mundane buildings that provide much less pleasure to their users and viewers. The same client who recognizes that quality in clothes, cars, and similar items costs more, can impose budgets for his buildings that bear little or no respect to the requirement of quality.

In many cases, especially where public funds are involved, only the initial cost concerns the instigator of the project, the subsequent running and maintenance costs being ignored until only a few years later these return to haunt those concerned. In Britain in the 1950s, 1960s and early 1970s the quantity of public buildings, rather than quality, seemed to be the prime concern of government, both central and local. Whilst there were some outstanding successes where these two apparently unresolvable and conflicting factors were indeed resolved and a few cases where quality ruled over quantity and buildings of a very high standard were constructed, the bulk of the buildings built did not unite quality and quantity.

It is probably wise to remember that some of our best loved buildings of the past cost far more than their original budgets—St Paul's Cathedral in London cost about double the original budget. Initial cost is usually the first thing that is forgotten about a building. Nevertheless, it is up to the design team to produce the building within the reasonable economic constraints that have been imposed. Simplicity of design has already been mentioned as the principal way of achieving this and designs should reflect it in their planning, form, shape, structure, choice of materials, and components, as well as in the services installations.

Planning should be straightforward and should be contained wherever possible in a simple shape; square or rectangular shapes are more economical to build than more complex shapes such as the 'L' or 'T', crucifix, star, circular, or free. Again, the nearer to square that the rectangular shape is, the more economical it is because of the lower ratio of external wall area to plan area. Thus the maximum floor area can be achieved for the minimum cost in buildings where a square plan is adopted. Of course the minimum external wall to floor ratio will be achieved with a circular plan but circles are expensive to construct and thus any saving in wall area is quickly lost in the complexity of the construction.

The height of building will have considerable impact on its form and also on the cost. In domestic buildings it is usually found that the traditional height for the locality proves to be the most economic because of the familiarity of the building team with the construction and working method. Thus whilst two-storey houses usually prove to be the most economic in Britain (even ignoring land costs), in Australia for instance, where the tradition is of single-storey dwellings, these prove to be the more economic.

That having been said, two-storey buildings for other uses tend to be more expensive than single-storey. A comparison can be made between a single-storey square building 10 m × 10 m and a two storey building 16.33 mm × 3 m both giving 100 m² of floor space. The latter building could cost as much as 26 per cent more than the former.

For buildings to function properly the plan shape will be determined by use (see Chapter 6) and certain plan shapes and sizes have developed that balance economics and function. In his book *Building Economics*, for instance, I. H. Seeley cites the desirable depth of office buildings as about 12 m which permits easy division into smaller units. However, single occupiers have usually been happy with 15 m depths whilst in America and Australia 18 m has been found to be acceptable. In hotels, it has been found that an economical arrangement is one where there are forty to fifty bedrooms per floor.

Circulation space is expensive but cannot be dispensed with and here Seeley suggests that providing this does not exceed about 19 per cent of gross floor area in offices and 21 per cent in four-storey flats these buildings will not suffer from an uneconomic excess of this type of space.

The most economic height of buildings other than houses depends upon a number of different factors, mainly construction/structure, services installations, and vertical transportation. Generally cost increases fairly rapidly as the number of storeys increases over about three. Nowadays four-storey buildings usually require lifts and/or escalators, construction becomes more complex both in its design and its execution (framed structures usually being employed rather than one incorporating walls and partitions which provide a dual function of enclosure and loadbearing), fire precautions become more complex and services installations are more elaborate. As the height of a building increases there are definite points where the costs rise rapidly. These are where the structural method has to change (as at the point where a frame is needed rather than loadbearing walls); where the foundations have to change from pad or strip to pile; where first and subsequent lifts are required (in flats one lift is required in a four-storey building and a second at seven-storeys); where additional fire protection and fire-fighting equipment are needed; where the more sophisticated services and structure require additional consult- ants to be added to the design team, and where more expensive plant (for example, tower cranes) are required for the construction. As the height of a building increases a greater proportion of the floor area is taken up with circulation, structure, and services. In addition, maintenance costs usually increase with height.

As with plans, the form of a building has as great an impact upon the economics as does the shape of the component parts. Simple cubes and rectangular prisms are the most economic forms (but not necessarily the more desirable aesthetically, see Chapter 7). This is because construction is easier as almost all materials and compo- nents come in rectolinear shapes or are designed for use with recto- linear shapes. Even plastic materials such as concrete require form- work which is easier to provide for rectolinear shapes than for either curved or free shapes. There are, of course, exceptions such as tensile structures clad in thin membranes or sprayed concrete but these rarely prove to be economic except for some special structures such as sports stadiums. Square and rectangular shapes for components usually prove to be the most economic and, wherever possible, standard products should always be used. Specials can prove to be disproportionately expensive and it is such a pity that, so often, standard building components are poorly designed in themselves and give the impression that the design has been produced to suit the manufacturing machine rather than the other way around.

The construction of a building is usually more economic if it follows the tried and tested methods employed in that place for buildings of that type. New innovations in construction are, of course, necessary otherwise there would be no progress. However, when it comes to economical building it is wise to let the other person do the experimenting and for the design team only to adopt it when the new methods or materials have been found satisfactory for their particular building type and in that locality.

Generally speaking, it is more economical to use walls and partitions as loadbearing elements on buildings up to three or four storeys. For buildings above this height a framed structure usually proves to be more economic depending upon the use of the building. The answer to the question of whether concrete or steel is more economic for the frame tends to vary from country to country. In Europe (including Britain) concrete seems to be the more economic whilst in the USA steel often proves to be better. On the other hand, single-storey industrial buildings, in which large clear spaces are required, are invariably more economic if built using a steel frame; this is because of the speed of erection together with the fact that the steel rarely needs any fire protection for this type of building.

Any form of construction that requires a high degree of precision in its execution will invariably prove to be more costly—not only because of the time factor and difficulty but also because of the chance of error and the cost of rectification if such errors were to occur. For this reason even the flat roof, which according to all the other rules quoted hitherto relating to simplicity of form and shape should invariably prove to be more economical than a pitched roof rarely proves to be the case, even in the initial construction. The possible exception to this is in the case of small domestic garages and extensions to existing buildings where the roof construction could prove to be extremely complex if pitches were incorporated that married up with the existing roof (see Chapter 8).

In buildings over one storey design teams should aid the construction by planning wide open spaces, where structural obstructions in the form of columns must be avoided, on the top floors whilst ensuring that the heaviest loading is on the ground floor or, at the very least, on the lower floors; this will simplify the structure and thus keep costs down.

The construction of the external envelope of a building, which is that part that contributes most to the external aesthetic, needs

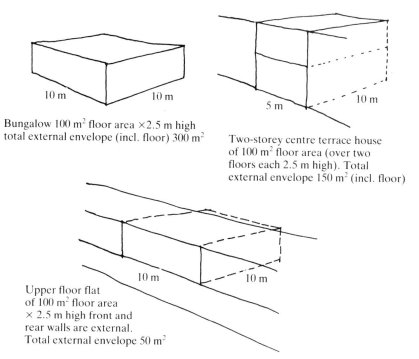

Bungalow 100 m² floor area ×2.5 m high
total external envelope (incl. floor) 300 m²

Two-storey centre terrace house
of 100 m² floor area (over two
floors each 2.5 m high). Total
external envelope 150 m² (incl. floor)

Upper floor flat
of 100 m² floor area
× 2.5 m high front and
rear walls are external.
Total external envelope 50 m²

*Figure 25   Various forms of domestic buildings showing the extent
of the external envelope through which heat is lost.*

careful consideration. Materials in common use in the locality will
usually prove to be the cheapest but even within the general range
choices will have to be made. Even for the humble brick prices can
vary by as much as a factor of 10 with the dearest rarely being the best
or the cheapest being the worst. Many other factors such as colour,
texture, strength, weathering, and so on will determine the choice of
bricks rather than the cost. The external envelope will have to take
the full force of the climatic and environmental factors and if careful
detailing and choice of materials does not take place the building will
quickly deteriorate requiring considerable expenditure over the years
on maintenance. This may soon overtake, in cost terms, any savings
that were made at the time of building.

The energy consumption of buildings for heating or cooling
amounts to a very large proportion of the total energy requirements of
most developed countries today. In Britain buildings account for 50
per cent of the country's energy consumption. As the current replacement rate of buildings in Britain is less than 1 per cent any impact of
new design on the nation's energy bill is going to be small but on the

budget of the occupiers all improvements incorporated at the design stage will be of help. This energy is now very expensive and no designer can consider that he has produced an economical building unless it is also energy efficient. Factors that affect the consumption of energy in buildings relate basically to whether the full implications of climatic design have been appreciated and implemented (see Chapter 3) so that the building is orientated in the best way and has its openings properly located to minimize heat loss/gain etc. In addition the envelope is required to provide a maximum of insulation against this heat loss/gain (except in some regions where high diurnal temperature ranges exist). In addition to the correct choice of materials and the provision of adequate insulation heat loss/gain can be affected by the shape of a building. Obviously the greater the ratio of external envelope to floor area the greater will be the heat loss. Figure 25 shows different shapes and types of domestic buildings all with the same floor area from which the more economical building can be identified from the point of view of energy consumption, assuming the same insulation qualities of the various elements of the envelope. Alex Gordon's plea as President of the Royal Institute of British Architects in 1972 that buildings should be designed so as to be long-life, loose-fit and low-energy is still as applicable as ever.

Legal

It is not the intention of this book to set out all the legal constraints that apply to buildings even in Britain, far less in other parts of the world, but to draw the student's attention to just how *certain* legal constraints have affected building design in the past and how others can affect design today.

Legal constraints have applied to building design and construction almost ever since man started to build 'permanent' buildings of any consequence and in London, apart from requirements during the Roman period, regulations have existed since AD 1189. The principal regulations, however, came after the Fire of London in 1666 and took the form of the London Building Act of 1667 which, naturally, was mainly concerned with preventing a repetition of the disastrous event of the previous year. This Act was the forerunner of other acts the most far-reaching of which was, probably, the 1774 London Building Act. This, together with the 1667 Act, possibly had more influence on building control in the English-speaking world than any others.

Almost all countries now have some form of building control but the regulations vary quite considerably from place to place—and even within individual countries because national building regulations are far from being the norm. In fact, it was as recently as 1966 that a national set of regulations came into being for England and Wales (excepting Inner London). Separate but similar regulations apply to Scotland and Northern Ireland. In countries where no national regulations exist the controlling authority is often the local council and the quality of these regulations can vary quite considerably. In rural areas these are often based on those that exist in the major centres of population of the country concerned where, for obvious reasons, building control is more important. In countries once under British rule it is not uncommon for the regulations to bear a marked resemblance to some of the older London Building Acts.

Building regulations are primarily concerned with protecting the health and safety of the users of the buildings directly involved, and of adjacent buildings, and as such are concerned with such things as structural stability, damp prevention, appropriate use of materials, prevention of spread of fire, and safety of occupants in case of fire, together with the provision of adequate light, air, and sanitation for the occupants. In addition regulations often extend to sound and thermal insulation for certain types of buildings whilst regulations applicable to larger buildings and buildings in multi-occupation usually have special requirements. The external appearance of buildings is often affected by building regulations and this has probably never been more noticeable than in eighteenth-century London where the Building Act of 1707 required that party walls extend for 18 in. (450 mm) above the roof of terraced houses and forbad the use of overhanging timber and plaster cornices recommending that parapets be provided and positively requiring these to extend 2 ft (600 mm) above a garret floor. The character of London's skyline was thus confirmed. In many other parts of Britain this projecting party wall is not usual although a few authorities adopted similar requirements and in some cases the London fashion was adopted. 12,000 miles away in Sydney in the nineteenth century this regulation was imposed and the skyline of Sydney's terraces bears a much closer resemblance to those of London than do those of Liverpool (see Plates 11, 24 and 37).

In the present day the appearance of buildings can still be affected by building regulations especially those relating to the spread of fire, as in the 1707 case. Back-up walls are often required behind glazed spandrels to prevent fire leap. In addition there can be restrictions on the use of less fire-resistant materials on the facade of buildings especially where these materials would be close to site boundaries.

Apart from the constraints imposed by the various building regulations, many countries operate a system of planning control whereby the type and use of a building together with its positioning and aesthetics can be fairly rigorously controlled. In Britain the current planning controls date from 1947 although attempts to restrict the spread of London date from much earlier. In the latter part of the sixteenth century Elizabeth I issued a proclamation which had as its principal aim the containment of the city to its then boundaries.

It is, of course, effects of legislation on the actual building that concerns us here. Depending upon the strength of the legislation and its enforcement, planning officers can exert considerable pressure on the designer not only in the materials that are used but also on the location of the building on the site, the style of the building, its fenestration, roof form and covering together with the location of entrances and exits for both vehicular and pedestrian traffic. Planners can also concern themselves with the number and location of parking spaces and landscaping as well as ensuring that the building use complies with the policies of their local plans. Where buildings are proposed in a conservation area in Britain applications will be carefully vetted and where alterations or demolition of a listed building are proposed additional consents are required. Most countries are now very conscious of their historic buildings and some form of legislation has been enacted to protect these against demolition or insensitive alteration or extension. Thus it can be seen that planning legislation can pose considerable constraints on the design team involved in producing a scheme for a new building or for the extension and alteration of an existing one. Early consultation with planning officers is always wise in all but the few places where a *laissez-faire* attitude still prevails (some newly developing countries and some parts of the USA). Where a planning officer's requirements appear to be unduly restrictive there are usually provisions for appeal and thus there is an in-built safeguard against the worst excesses of planning conditions.

In addition to building and planning control there are many other legal constraints applicable to buildings of particular types and uses —again usually to protect the users from health and other hazards. Contained within other legislation affecting particular industries and employments there are often requirements relating to the buildings used for such activities—for example, legislation affecting shops and offices which among other things sets out, in most cases, minimum requirements for toilet facilities for staff together with lunch spaces and other amenities. Similar legislation also exists in many places for factories and other buildings where people are employed. Requirements of licensing authorities for places of entertainment and places where liquor is sold often dictate fire precautions and toilet accommodation as well as other minimum standards with which buildings must comply. In Britain all but the smallest hotels and lodging houses require a fire certificate before they can operate. To obtain this, a very high standard of fire precautions must be provided. Special requirements usually exist wherever food is handled, and these vary from hand-washing facilities to insect screening and often include requirements for materials and constructional details.

Thus it can be seen that the designer of a building must be aware of all the legislation that applies to his particular building and must ensure that the finished product complies in every respect. In many cases this will require a compromise as do so many of the constraints outlined in this and the preceding chapters.

Conclusion

The ever-increasing complexity of technology and services together with the general increase in noise levels and legislation combined with the ever-pressing need to provide an economical solution to a building problem means that the design team needs to be constantly aware of the constraints and challenges that it faces from these sources. A proper balance between the conflicting requirements will be essential for a good building.

References

Alder, J. *Mitchell's Guide to Services Selection and Integration in low Rise Buildings* (Batsford: London, 1983).

British Standards Institute CP3: Chapter III: 1972 *Sound Insulation and Noise Reduction* (BSI: London, 1972).

Burberry, P. *Mitchell's Building Construction: Environment and Services* (Batsford: London, 1978).

Cowan, H. J. *Structural Systems* (Van Nostrand Reinhold: New York, 1981).

Everett, A. *Mitchell's Building Construction: Materials* (Batsford: London, 1983).

Foster, J. S. *Mitchell's Building Construction: Structure and Fabric Part I* (Batsford: London, 1979).

Foster, J. S. *Mitchell's Building Construction: Structure and Fabric Part II* (Batsford: London, 1983).

Hodgkinson, A. *Architects Journal Handbook of Building Structure* (Architectural Press: London, 1974).

King, H. and Everett, A. *Mitchell's Building Construction: Components and Finishes* (Batsford: London, 1971).

Seeley, I. H. *Building Economics: An Appraisal and Control of Building Design and Cost* (Macmillan: London, 1983).

Speaight, A. and Stone, G. *Architects Journal Legal Handbook: The Law for Architects* (Architectural Press: London, 1982).

6

Planning

Introduction

It may be argued that the most important job of the designer of buildings is the planning of the same, but this is most certainly an understatement. The planning of the building is of the utmost importance but the marriage between the plan and the external appearance and all that this implies is where the true work of art materializes. It is possible to produce a building where the plan works like a machine but where the building does not provide that element of delight that is so important. Conversely it is also possible to produce a superb building from an aesthetic point of view but one which does not 'work'.

Flexibility

The rapid changes that are taking place in society today, especially in the communications sphere, can often render a building's layout obsolete before that building is more than a few years old, or even—in some circumstances—before it is completed and commissioned, such is the time-lag in construction. It is therefore essential that all buildings are designed to be as flexible as possible and to enable them to be adapted and altered to suit changing needs easily and economically. There are buildings that have to be designed and built to suit a particular function or process—especially in the industrial sphere —where it is not possible to build in flexibility, but these cases are rare and usually the plant or process contained therein is so expensive that the building itself only represents a fraction of the total cost of the project. It is therefore more practicable to demolish and rebuild when the process becomes obsolete than to alter and adapt.

88

Optimization of space

Buildings are usually built to house human beings and to protect them from the elements whilst they carry out certain activities. It follows that for a building to function properly it is essential that the design team fully understands the activity that is to be performed and how this may best be accommodated.

Planning is concerned with the optimization of space in buildings and whilst it is rare for there to be no waste space in a building any waste space should be kept to a minimum. One area that is often associated with waste space is circulation space—foyers, lobbies, and passages. It is rarely possible to exclude these entirely from any scheme whilst in others it is possible to find a dual use for these spaces (for example using theatre foyers as bars and exhibition spaces). In order to appreciate the maximization of space to its fullest it is worth studying examples from other industries, all of which have been designed, in most cases, within much tighter space controls that exist in buildings. Accommodation in transport vehicles is a case in point. The galley in a launch or airline has to cope with many of the same functions as a kitchen in the average house whilst a ship's cabin or railway sleeper is the same as a bedroom. Figure 26(a) shows the plan of a 'roomette' on a New South Wales Railways train which acts as a sitting room, bedroom and toilet for one person. No-one would suggest that this would be a suitable environment for everyday living. However it is possible to see from these examples, where space is at an absolute premium, just how this space can be maximized by carefully analysing all activities and synthesizing them into a solution. Wherever possible spaces should be able to be used for more than one activity (see Figure 27).

Anthropometrics and ergonomics

In order to appreciate just how much space is required for humans to carry out certain activities it is necessary to make use of the study of anthropometrics which is the study of human dimensions—sizes, weights and range of movements. These include not only the static dimensions for persons standing, sitting or lying but also dynamic dimensions which enable the designer to take into account the space needed to allow for movement. These dimensions are readily available and are generally based on the active adult. Dimensions are also available for special categories of people such as children, the elderly and the disabled. Dimensions are normally accepted if they apply to

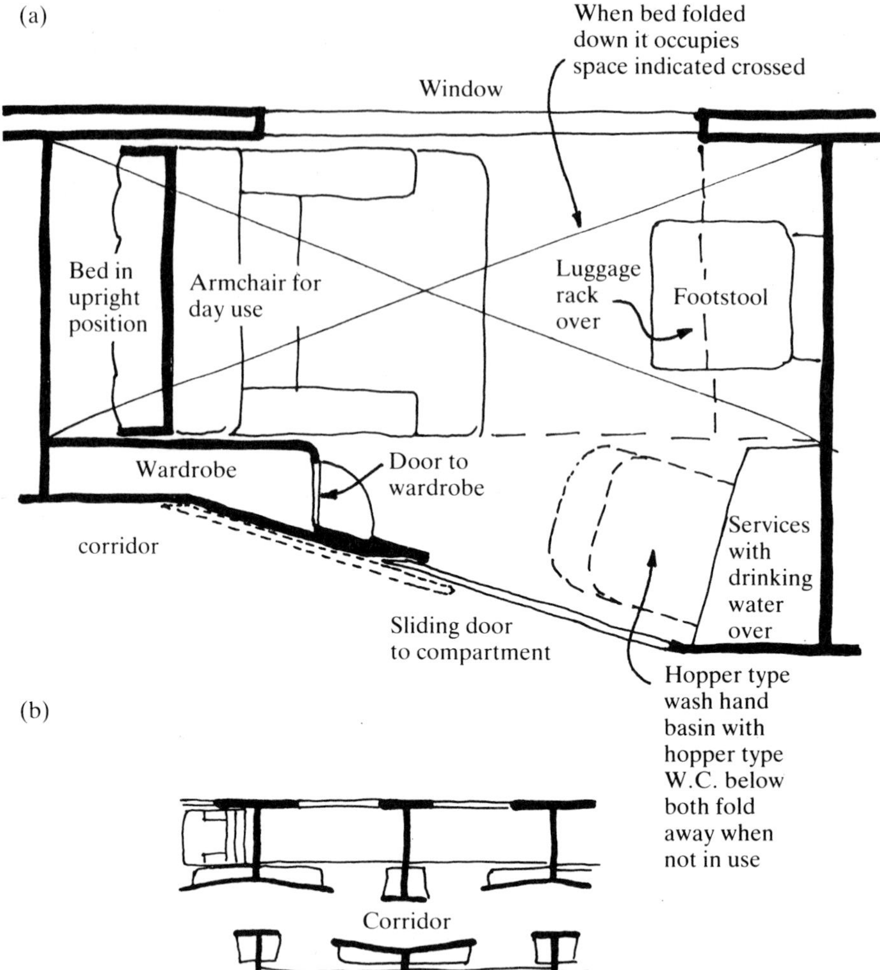

(a)

When bed folded
down it occupies
space indicated crossed

Window

Bed in
upright
position

Armchair for
day use

Luggage
rack
over

Footstool

Wardrobe

Door to
wardrobe

corridor

Services
with
drinking
water
over

Sliding door
to compartment

Hopper type
wash hand
basin with
hopper type
W.C. below
both fold
away when
not in use

(b)

Corridor

*Figure 26   Single berth sleeping compartment (roomette) in use on
New South Wales Railways: (a) plan of compartment; (b) part plan of
carriage. (Adapted from drawings supplied by courtesy of State
Railway Authority of New South Wales.)*

90–95 per cent of the category of person for which the design is to
cater. Nevertheless, for certain categories it is necessary to strive for a
higher percentage.

Anthropometrics can be extended into the field of ergonomics,

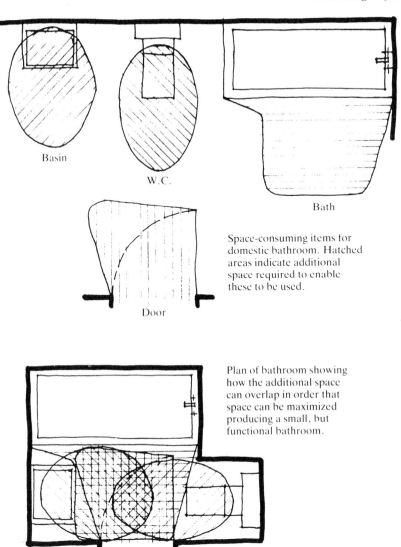

Basin

W.C.

Bath

Space-consuming items for
domestic bathroom. Hatched
areas indicate additional
space required to enable
these to be used.

Door

Plan of bathroom showing
how the additional space
can overlap in order that
space can be maximized
producing a small, but
functional bathroom.

Figure 27   Maximization of space in a domestic bathroom.

which is the scientific study of people with their working environ-
ments. It goes beyond anthropometrics not only in that it concerns
itself with tools and equipment but it also involves behavioural
psychology together with technologies and disciplines.

The designer will employ anthropometrical data in the designing of spaces (see Figure 27), calculating areas, determining widths of corridors, pitches of stairs, and arranging layouts. In addition, this data helps with determining heights of benches and shelves, locating windows and doors as well as the location of controls such as window catches and locks.

Zoning

In order to understand the planning process within a building it is, perhaps, best to start with a building with which most readers will be familiar—the single-family house. Because of its familiarity many people assume that planning a house is a simple task but this is not the case and the more restrictions which are imposed by site, climate, legislation etc. the greater the problems.

The activities of a house can basically be divided into two broad areas or zones; those associated with the day time and those associated with the night time. The average house is divided into these two zones and the two-storey house effectively isolates, yet links, these zones. The zones are the living zone, usually located on the ground floor in two-storey houses and the sleeping zone normally found on the first floor. The living zone contains sitting room, dining spaces, kitchen, utility or laundry room, garage, outdoor area, garden storage, cloakrooms and so on, whilst the sleeping zone usually contains bedrooms, bathrooms and toilet facilities together with associated storage.

In order to fully appreciate this separation of activities it is a good idea to start to think where certain items should be stored in a typical two-storey house assuming that rare commodity—an abundance of storage space. Where, for instance, should the suitcases be kept? Because suitcases are usually packed in bedrooms where clothes are stored their logical storage space should be in bedrooms, but what of, say, a picnic basket? This should ideally be stored in the kitchen whilst medicines which so often have to be taken with water and are usually linked to meals should really be kept in the kitchen (in a child-proof locker) and not in the bathroom where they are most commonly found.

These day and night zones could also be classified as noisy and quiet, active and passive. Whichever way we classify the activities we will come out at much the same result, (for example, bedroom —sleeping, night, quiet, passive; kitchen—living, day, noisy, active). Other activities are more difficult to classify under these headings —even the living room which is obviously going to be within the living zone and is basically associated with daytime (including evening); but is it always noisy or quiet and does it contain active or passive activities? This immediately throws up one of the dilemmas of planning. If everyone in the house wanted to do the same activities at the same time then the single living room would work and providing it was designed for the worst case—which is noisy and active—all would be well, but where there is more than one person living in a house (and in Britain that is the case for approximately 75 per cent of households) different people may wish to pursue different interests simultaneously. It is therefore wise, where space permits, to provide for separate living rooms so that one member of the household can pursue quiet activities whilst the rest follow noisy ones. This may require bedrooms for teenagers to be considered as bed-sitting rooms and hence be re-classified from a zoning point of view.

As has been mentioned above the single-family house divides itself into two zones fairly easily but there are a number of 'bridging' activities. Take clothes washing for instance. Where a separate laundry or utility room is not provided this activity is usually performed in the kitchen—no doubt as a left over from the days of boiling clothes over the kitchen range and drying them outside. Nowadays in the developed world most households use washing machines and many dry their clothes by machine indoors. If this is the way the clothes are to be washed and dried then the kitchen is not the correct place for this activity. Dirty clothes are removed in the bedroom or bathroom, soiled bed linen and towels are all produced from the bedroom or bathroom which only leaves the small quantity of washing produced at table plus teatowels being produced in the living zone. After washing, drying and ironing the bulk of the washing will be stored in the sleeping zone. From this analysis of the washing process we can see that there is a good argument for including the clothes-washing facilities in the bathroom area. In Britain it is not possible to have electrical equipment in the bathroom itself (although this is permitted in some countries) thus it may be best to provide a clothes washing space adjacent to the bathroom. Naturally this would be less than desirable in two—(or more) storey houses if ironing was still done in (say) the kitchen or if clothes were dried outside. Nevertheless, from the above discussion it is apparent that it is necessary to analyse each activity in the brief, to relate it to other activities and then to locate it in the most appropriate zone of the building.

For buildings other than domestic ones, zoning can be quite complex. If we were to consider a hotel, for instance, the noisy and quiet zones must be much more carefully analysed. In addition there are public zones where everyone has access—foyers, bars, restaurants, car parks and so on, then there are the semi-public areas restricted to guests and their invited friends—bedrooms, lounges, and perhaps special dining rooms. After this there are the zones restricted to staff, especially the service zones such as kitchens, laundries, staff quarters, offices and so on. Finally, there is the private zone for the owner or manager and his family. Hotel policy will determine much of the distinction between public and semi-public. However, it will then be up to the design-team to ensure that it is easy to separate the zones whilst coping with all the other planning problems which are discussed later.

In some buildings such a degree of security must exist in one or more parts that it must not be possible to pass from one zone to another without authorization. An example of this would be in an air terminal where access to duty-free shops is restricted to outward bound passengers. This area needs careful zoning and rigid separation together with the necessary control barriers and passes (in this case a boarding card) before any person can enter. In certain organizations the security and separation is essential to protect valuables (both materially and informationally, such as computers) as is the case in banks.

After the requirements have been analysed from a zoning point of view it is possible to consider flow and circulation.

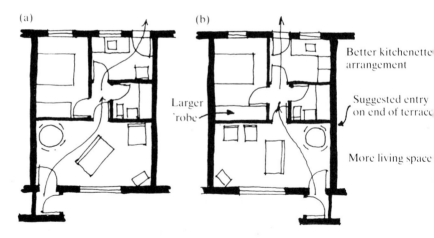

(a)   (b)

Larger 'robe

Better kitchenette arrangement

Suggested entry on end of terrace

More living space

Figure 28   'Spec' built 'starter' house showing how modifications to positioning of doors enable a maximization of working and living space by reducing circulation space: (a) as proposed; (b) minor modifications.

Flow and circulation

The circulation of people and objects through buildings varies in importance from one building to another. In buildings such as houses this aspect of planning will often be compromised in order to satisfy other design requirements. Nevertheless it can be seen from Figure 28 that a careful analysis of the circulation in a small domestic building followed by minor changes in the positioning of doors can reduce the space required for this activity and, as result, maximize working and living space. Wherever possible, living spaces and kitchen should not be criss-crossed by circulation routes. In other building types such as hospitals or airports circulation is of paramount importance. In the latter case not only must the flow of passengers be considered but also the movement of luggage, staff, goods for restaurants, bars, duty-free sales and other shops, cars, taxis, buses, refuse and a host of other vital services before beginning to consider the circulation problems associated with the planes themselves—their servicing and operation, security and quarantine.

One of the aids that the design team may use in solving the circulation problems of a building is to use flow or bubble diagrams, which enable an analysis to be made of the principal circulation routes and the relationship of spaces one with another. Figure 29 shows a 'flow diagram' for a four-bedroom family house from which it can be seen that even in this 'simple' example the circulation patterns

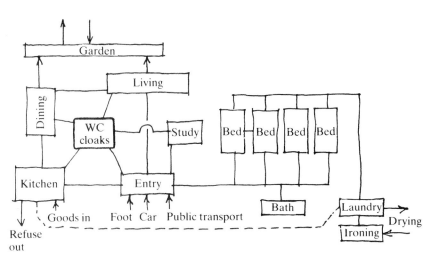

Figure 29 *'Flow diagram' of family house.*

can be fairly complex. The zoning of the house mentioned earlier also starts to emerge more clearly. From the circulation pattern the very beginnings of a plan start to emerge. Add to this the room sizes desired, orientate the plan to comply with the site analysis (see Chapter 4) and a tentative solution is beginning to emerge. In this example it may be noted that certain circulation routes cross one another and are therefore in conflict; in this case, this may not matter but in other building types it is essential that there is not conflict between certain flows.

Figure 30 shows a flow diagram for an airport terminal in a simplified form. Here it is essential that there is no conflict (say) between luggage flowing to the planes and rubbish leaving the restaurant or between the 'meeters and greeters' and the 'in transit' passengers. Another advantage of the flow diagram is that it enables the designer to see where different level separation may be advisable. In the airport example we see that by introducing this it is possible to keep arrivals on a separate level from departures which is common practice in larger airports. Different levels also enable administration to be separately zoned and yet to have the necessary circulation to other parts of the building. Luggage too can flow from 'check-in' to plane and from plane to 'collect' at separate levels. Flow diagrams

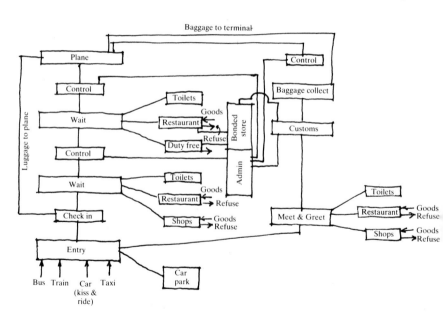

Figure 30 *'Flow diagram' for airport building (simplified version).*

enable the design team to see where the most appropriate location is for vertical circulation (stairs, lifts and/or escalators). It is also possible to indicate quantity of flow which will aid the designer to determine width of corridors and stairs, number of doors, lifts, etc.

Security

It is unfortunate that in this day and age the designer has to pay so much attention to this particular aspect of planning which is essential in all building types. It is possible to improve the security of the occupants of a building and its contents by security-conscious planning. In buildings where valuable goods are stored or processed (for example, banks) then zoning will be used to separate high-security areas from those to which the public has access—everyone is familiar with the security barriers and grills that separate us as bank customers from the tellers and other staff handling money. Without proper planning from the beginning this would not be easy to implement.

It was the American, Oscar Newman, who first used the phrase 'defensible space' in relation to the design of buildings. Mr Newman was particularly concerned with housing estates and, although some writers and researchers have discredited his methods in recent times, the conclusions that he reached and put into practice in the USA have proved to be successful in combatting the problem of lack of security on certain public housing schemes. Oscar Newman's thesis is really a re-statement of Jane Jacob's principle espoused about a quarter of a century earlier of 'eyes on the street'.

The principle behind these theses is that buildings should be designed in such a way that they police themselves. Figure 31 shows some plans of housing developments that work from this point of view and some that do not. In all cases where entrances are not exposed to the scrutiny of residents in the development it would be relatively easy for an intruder to attack and break into the buildings unobserved—this would not be so easy in the case of those examples where there are 'eyes on the street'.

Buildings with too many entrances and exits are also difficult to make secure. From a security point of view buildings should only have one, or at most, two entrances. However, this may not be possible in large and complex buildings because of problems of workability including zoning and circulation whilst in many other buildings the requirements of fire officers will result in 'means of escape' provisions which in many cases are directly opposed to those necessary to provide a secure building. It is the duty of the design

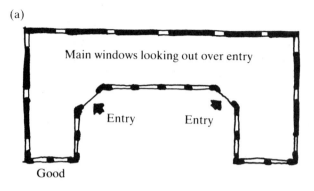

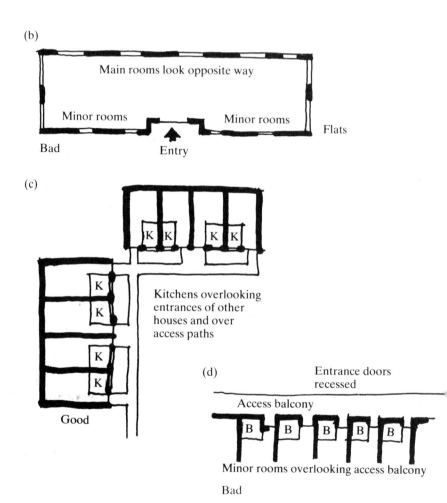

Figure 31   Plans of flats and houses showing good and bad examples of 'eyes on the street': (a) good flats, (b) bad flats: (c) good houses; (d) bad flats with balconies.

team to produce a scheme that copes with all the conflicting requirements. This will mean the employment of other aids such as panic bolts which can be fitted to doors enabling people to escape from a building easily in an emergency but do not allow intruders to enter from the outside.

Nowadays many electronic devices are also available, enabling buildings to be rendered more secure but these are expensive and where the design team can produce plan forms that satisfactorily do the same job without recourse to these items a better building must be produced.

Means of escape

Requirements for means of escape in the case of fire vary considerably from one part of the world to another and even within countries different authorities can impose differing requirements on designers. The main principle of means of escape is that the occupants of a building should be able to vacate that building within a safe period of time after the alarm has been given that an emergency has arisen. The emergency usually being considered is that of fire, but nowadays the design team must also bear in mind other emergencies such as terrorist bombs which will have a different effect upon the building's structure than a fire.

Means of escape requirements vary from building type to building type and are also related to the construction of the building and its fire separation (see also Chapter 5) as well as the finishes employed especially within escape routes. The increased use of plastics in buildings has led to new problems of toxic fumes being given off which can be far more serious in disabling or killing those attempting to escape than smoke or the actual fire itself. It is therefore vital that the design team takes all these matters into consideration when designing a building.

The occupants of a building must be carefully considered when designing for evacuation of the building. A group of active teenagers in a recreation centre will be able to escape much more rapidly than (say) a group of elderly people in the same building and this difference becomes even more acute when the occupants are asleep or disabled either permanently or temporarily as would be the case in a hospital. People unfamiliar with their surroundings, such as guests in a hotel or visitors to other establishments, will all take longer to escape. The code of practice published in Britain by the British Standards Institution takes these factors into account and is a valuable guide for any designer. However, it is the designer's responsibility to ensure that his building is safe for its occupants and in many cases he will have to decide to go much further than the basic requirements or regulations in force. It is good to be aware of requirements in other countries and in other parts of the same country as these can be very useful especially if the requirements of the controlling authority for your building are a little on the light side. Clients may require convincing, especially if the designer exceeds minimum requirements, which will inevitably cost more money. The British requirements in general, and those applicable to Greater London—in particular, are felt to be of a high standard.

Planning for services

As buildings have become more complex over recent years services have played an increasing part. Not only do we have to cope with water supply and drainage but buildings also have to incorporate heating and/or cooling, lighting, telephone and increasingly more complex communication services in the information technology sphere. Apart from the actual outlet provisions for all of these services, which must be carefully considered, the services need space in which to run. All too often inadequate space for service runs is provided leading to inefficient, cramped and noisy installations with no room for alteration and adaptation at a later date.

From the very outset the design team must provide adequate space for service runs through its building. This space needs to be provided both vertically and horizontally and separate ducts must be provided where services can interfere with one another such as electricity and television cables. Service ducts need to be easily accessible for maintenance work without disrupting decorations and finishes. As most services begin to wear out within 15 to 25 years they should be capable of being renewed without undue disruption. New services may well have to be introduced into buildings during their lifetime and one has only to look back 100 years (the average life of most buildings except those standing on very valuable sites such as downtown Manhattan) to see the changes in services that can occur in a building. The basic principle to remember when planning for services is that you can never be too generous in space allocation.

Planning to minimize energy consumption

In Chapter 3 the concept of maximizing the benefits of the climate in order to minimize energy consumption is discussed and the importance of positioning rooms and spaces in such a way that their orientation is suitable for use is stressed. In Chapter 5 the techno-logical constraints imposed by high energy costs was introduced. This high-energy cost must be considered in planning spaces to ensure compact plans which minimize external surfaces from which heat can escape in colder climates whilst in hot humid zones the flow of air through buildings will be the determining factor.

Heat sources should be located where they can be of maximum benefit. Lessons can be learnt in regard to this from simple vernacular buildings of the past. (see Figure 32).

Conclusion

The plan of a building should reflect the function of the building and the various constraints applicable to the particular case. It will invariably be a compromise but it must be the best under the circumstances with the design team balancing the constraints of climate, site, technology, legislation, and economics with flexibility, optimization of space, separation of activities, circulation, security, and means of escape whilst at all times bearing in mind the visual appearance of the finished product.

References

British Standards Institute CP3 Chapter III: 1972 *Sound Insulation & Noise Reduction* (BSI: London, 1972).

British Standards Institute CP3 Chapter IV: *Precautions against Fire Part 1*: 1971 Flats and maisonettes (in blocks over two storeys); *Part 2*: 1968 Shops and department stores; *Part 3*: 1968 Office buildings (BSI: London, 1968 and 1971).

Department of the Environment *DB24 Spaces in the Home Part 1*: Bathrooms and WCs; *Part 2*: Kitchen and laundry spaces (HMSO: London, 1980).

Department of the Environment *DB26 New Housing and Road Traffic Noise* (HMSO: London, 19).

Greater London Council *An Introduction to Housing Layouts* (Architectural Press: London, 1980).

Jacobs, J. *The Death and Life of Great American Cities* (Penguin: Harmondsworth, 1965).

Mills, E. D. (ed.) *Planning: Architects Technical Reference Data* (Newnes-Butterworths: London, 1977).

Newman, O. *Design Guidelines for Creating Defensible Space* National Institute of Law Enforcement and Criminal Justice, 1976).

Tutt, P. and Alder, D. *New Metric Handbook* (Architectural Press: London, 1979).

Underwood, G. *The Security of Buildings* (Architectural Press: London, 1984).

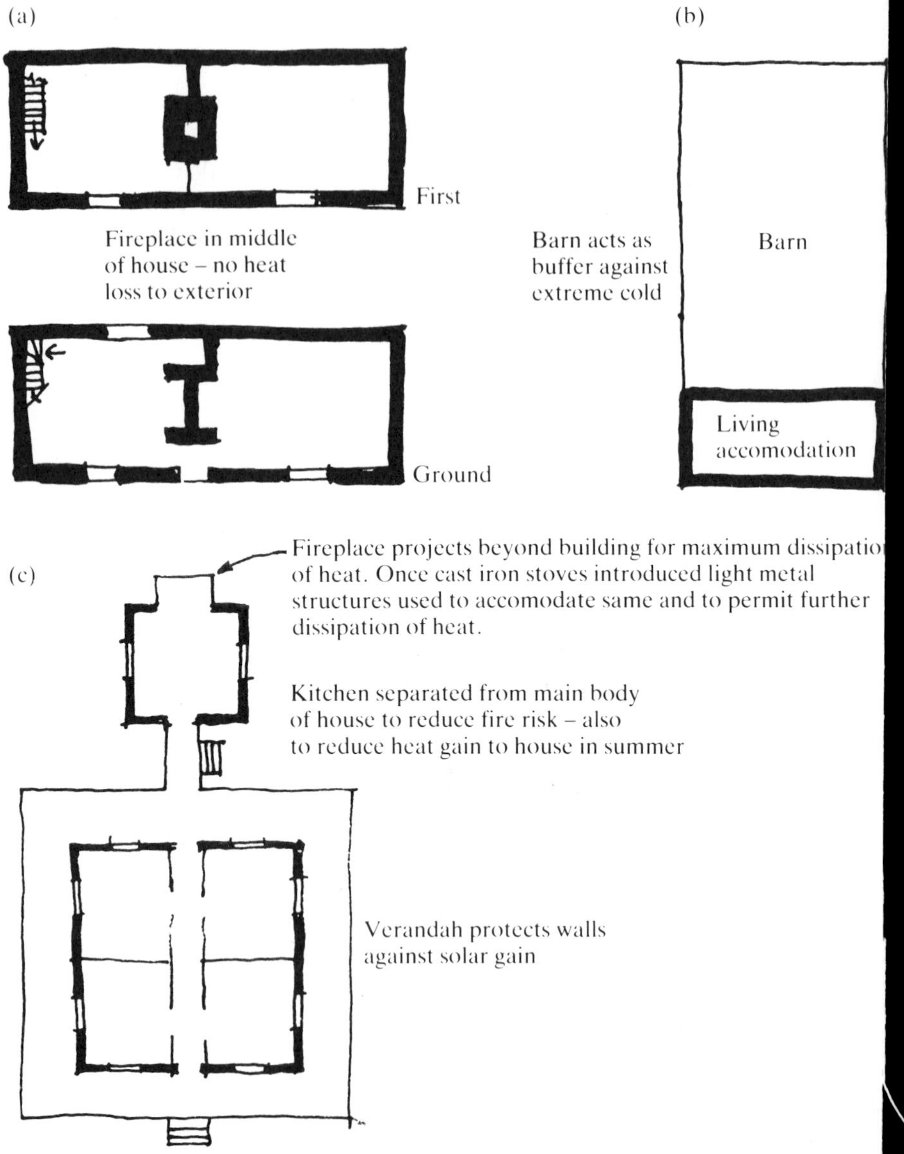

(a)

(b)

First

Fireplace in middle
of house – no heat
loss to exterior

Barn acts as
buffer against
extreme cold

Barn

Ground

Living
accomodation

Fireplace projects beyond building for maximum dissipatio[n]
of heat. Once cast iron stoves introduced light metal
structures used to accomodate same and to permit further
dissipation of heat.

(c)

Kitchen separated from main body
of house to reduce fire risk – also
to reduce heat gain to house in summer

Verandah protects walls
against solar gain

*Figure 32   Vernacular buildings planned to provide greater comfort
and to reduce energy consumption for heating/cooling: (a) plans of
vernacular cottage, south-east England, sixteenth to nineteenth
century; (b) plan of a farmhouse/barn in Alpine location; (c) vernacular cottage in Australia, nineteenth and early twentieth
century.*

7
Aesthetics

Introduction

It is upon the external appearance of buildings that most people base their judgement as to whether they like or dislike a particular building unless, of course it is a building that they use. However, the number of buildings that any one individual actually uses is very small compared with the number that form the backdrop to his or her activities. The few buildings that a person does use will come in for a much more detailed criticism by the user whilst the remainder will be judged by their external appearance as the sole criteria.

Whether a person reacts favourably to the exterior of a building will depend upon a number of factors about that person such as his or her age, cultural background, occupation, prejudices and so on. Nevertheless, a common thread of approval or disapproval will start to emerge. Some buildings will tend to be looked upon favourably whilst others will not be approved of by most people. There will be, of course, people who will not be particularly concerned one way or another but these people are fairly oblivious of their surroundings in any case.

Why do certain buildings receive general acclaim whilst others meet with disapproval? The answer lies, as it does in all arts, in whether the building's design fulfills certain generally accepted criteria. Buildings should observe certain rules of basic construction, planning, and aesthetics in the same way as a piece of literature or music. However, as in music and literature, this will not, in itself, mean that a work of art is the result. To produce the work of art something else must be added, which can best be described as an element of delight.

Buildings are perceived as a series of forms, shapes and lines and it is in the arrangement of these which determines whether the building produces a favourable appearance or otherwise.

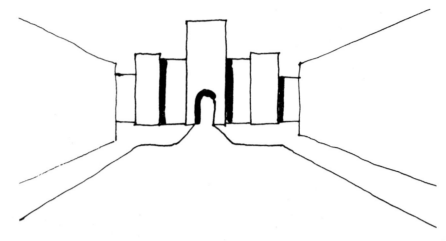

Figure 33   Processional route almost producing an elevational view.

Form

Buildings are invariably perceived in three dimensions and whilst the designer prepares true elevations of each wall it is extremely rare for any wall to be seen in true elevation. Occasionally where processional routes have been provided leading to major buildings an apparently two-dimensional view of the building is observed but even here perspective distorts especially where the building contains reveals or recesses (see Figure 33).

It is essential therefore for the full three-dimensional impact of a building to be considered not just from one vantage point but from many. Few designers are able to do this and to thus produce a building which is a three-dimensional delight. Patrick Nuttgens suggests that there have been very few architects who have achieved this and he asserts that these few include William of Sens at Canterbury Cathedral, Sir John Vanbrugh at Castle Howard, Yorks, Sir John Soane at the Bank of England, London, Sir Edwin Lutyens at Delhi and Le Corbusier at Ronchamp Chapel. It is by no means unusual for a building that looks very good from one position to look poor from another—this is especially true where a new vista is opened up by road improvements or other change to the surroundings. New open spaces have often distorted views and hence the perceived form of buildings (see Plates 17 and 18) which show the Brisbane City Hall, Queensland, comparing the views before and after an extended open

Plate 17 (left) City Hall, Brisbane, Queensland, 1930, before square extended and raised (T. R. Hall & G. G. Prentice). Photo courtesy of: Queensland Railways.

Plate 18 (right) City Hall, Brisbane, Queensland, 1930, after square extended and raised in 1975. Photo courtesy of: Brisbane City Council.

space was provided. The setting and background to a building makes a major contribution to the aesthetic quality of that building and also to the way in which the form is perceived. Buildings sited on the tops of hills show themselves in a more pronounced way than those located in a confined urban setting.

The form of a building is usually dictated by the spatial requirements of the building related to the site size and other design constraints including its construction and also the climatic zone in which it is built. (see Chapter 3). In a domestic house the form will be determined by the floor area required, the peculiarities of the site, the number of storeys desired and the construction and materials chosen for the building (for example, if tile or slates are chosen for a roof covering the roof will be pitched and thus the form will be quite different from a building where asphalt is chosen as a roof covering

Plate 19 Road Bridge across the Humber, 1981. Photo courtesy of: City of Kingston upon Hull.

Plate 20 L'Atelier Guitti, Antwerp, 1926 (Le Corbusier). Photo courtesy of: Julian Feary architects.

when a flat roof would result). Louis Sullivan's statement that 'form follows function' (see Chapter 1) was a reaction to the buildings forced into pseudo-classical or medieval form which were common in the latter part of the nineteenth century.

The eye is usually happier with simple forms—the cube, the rectangular prism, the pyramid, the sphere—and it does not like to be confused by forms that are not clear or by too many different forms. However, it does not like monotony either and thus very large simple forms tend to be disliked.

Certain forms are associated with particular buildings—triangular prisms or combinations of them are seen as providing shelter in parts of the world with climates that have reasonable precipitation, and thus pitched roof buildings are felt to be more 'homely' in those zones even although flat roofs are constructionally feasible. Religious buildings are especially associated with symbolic forms—domes, cones, pyramids, even hands clasped in prayer.

Unadorned structures often have the simplest forms and here civil engineers have produced superb examples where Sullivan's 'form

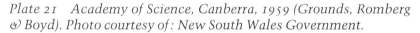

Plate 21   Academy of Science, Canberra, 1959 (Grounds, Romberg & Boyd). Photo courtesy of: New South Wales Government.

Plate 22   Casa Mila, Barcelona, 1907 (Antoni Gaudí). Photo courtesy of: Julian Feary architects.

follows function' is truly found. No excess material or ornament —just simple lines and shapes culminating in delightful graceful form. Plates 19–23 show buildings and structures of various forms. Plate 19 shows the simple unadorned structure of the Humber Road Bridge; Plate 20 shows a building of rectolinear form (L'Atelier Guitte, Antwerp); Plate 21 shows one of hemi-spherical form (Academy of Science Canberra); and Plates 22 and 23 show buildings employing free forms (Casa Mila, Barcelona and Sydney Opera House).

Shape

Although buildings are perceived in three dimensions certain parts of buildings (for example, windows and doors) are seen more in two

Plate 23   Opera House, Sydney, New South Wales 1959–1973 (J. Utzon). Photo courtesy of: New South Wales Government.

dimensions and here shape is important. Simple geometric shapes such as the square and rectangle are the more common—not least of all because these are the more economic to construct. However, circles (or part thereof, such as arches), triangles and certain free shapes have regularly been used to provide relief and contrast (see Plate 24, the Banquetting Hall in Whitehall). Some shapes are essentially functional; others may be provided for decorative purposes and this is often the case where circular, free and other complex shapes are employed. Shape is also closely allied with proportion which is discussed later.

Certain shapes are more assertive than others in drawing the eye to them (for example, squares and circles) and these can be used where a stop or pause is required on a façade. Shapes can also be used to

*Plate 24   Banquetting Hall, Whitehall, Greater London, 1616–1619
(Inigo Jones).*

provide rhythm and to emphasize the vertical or horizontal as in the
Banquetting Hall, Whitehall shown in Plate 24. Here the balustrade
at the top and the square windows at the bottom of façade act as stops
and the alternating triangular and segmental pediments over the
main windows provide rhythm.

Like form, certain shapes have symbolic associations (for example,
the pointed arch with the church) and it is thus important that shapes
that are chosen are appropriate and are clearly stated so that the eye is
not confused. A shape that is almost square is disturbing as the eye is
not sure whether it is seeing a square or a rectangle.

Shapes can be affected by shade and shadow, perspective or the
form of a building, especially where this is curved (see Plate 25, the
Royal Crescent in Bath). However, the eye tends to remain uncon-
fused providing shapes are repeated and regularly arranged.

Plate 25   Royal Crescent, Bath, Avon, 1767–1775 (John Wood the younger). Photo courtesy of: Bath City Council Leisure and Tourist Services.

The arrangement of shape is as important as the shapes themselves. The key here is to provide regularity without monotony and this can be achieved on large façades by grouping shapes together and ensuring that the spaces between the shapes are pleasant and complement the shapes themselves (see Figure 34).

Line

Shapes are made up of various lines—straight, curved, and free and these lines can be used to emphasize or subdue the visual effect. Lines have an emotional impact on the eye. Horizontal lines tend to be restful and can be used to emphasize the length of a building (see Plate 26 and Figure 35); vertical lines on tall buildings are stimulating and similarly can be used to emphasize verticality on a part or the whole of a building (see Plate 27 and Figure 35); inclined lines tend to be disturbing unless they relate to a specific function or structural

Monotony	Grouping of windows relieves monotony and can provide rhythm|

Figure 34   Windows on large façade.

component (see Plate 28). Where lines intersect they provide a centre of attraction and sometimes this can be given added emphasis as in the boss at the junction or ribs on a vaulted ceiling. Curved lines are usually soothing and can provide interest and rhythm.

Lines should always relate to structural or functional elements and should not simply be added to a façade for no apparent reason (such as a change of colour or material for no functional purpose).

Plate 26   Housing at Branch Hill, Hampstead, Greater London, 1978 (Benson & Forsyth for Director of Architecture and Surveying, London Borough of Camden). Photo courtesy of: London Borough of Camden Directorate of Architecture and Surveying.

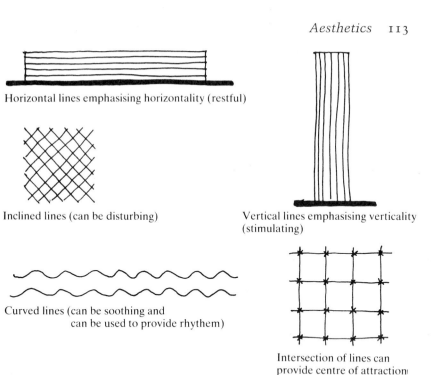

Horizontal lines emphasising horizontality (restful)

Inclined lines (can be disturbing)

Vertical lines emphasising verticality (stimulating)

Curved lines (can be soothing and can be used to provide rhythem)

Intersection of lines can provide centre of attraction

Figure 35   Lines on a building.

Plate 28   Hancock Building, Chicago, 1969 (Skidmore, Owings & Merrill). Photo courtesy of: Julian Feary architects.

Plate 27 City Hall, Toronto, Ontario 1964 (V. Revell). Photo courtesy of: B. T. F. Smith.

Architectural principles

In order to achieve a fine building (a piece of architecture) which gives delight it is necessary for these forms, shapes and lines to be chosen and arranged in a skilful and artistic way in order that the basic principles of architecture which are stability, convenience, and beauty can be exploited to the full.

Stability

The first of the basic principles of architecture is stability. A building that falls down is not going to be of much use to the client, nor is it going to contribute to the townscape. In the past, many buildings did in fact fall down, and it was through this falling down process that certain empirical methods of design and construction evolved. If a house or church tower collapsed, then another stronger one was built and if it collapsed it was rebuilt even stronger still until finally it did not collapse. Eventually scientific methods of design and construction were developed and nowadays, because of these scientific developments, the collapse of buildings is fairly rare, although of course it is by no means totally unknown.

Buildings are expected to be stable and the users of buildings have 100 per cent faith in the design and construction of buildings from this particular point of view. The same people who appreciate that there is some form of risk in travelling by motorcar, train or aeroplane, do not expect to be injured or killed in a building except as a result of some outside force such as earthquake, bomb, fire, or perhaps some mechanical breakdown such as lift failure.

Buildings must not only be stable themselves but they must also look stable and especially nowadays when most designs are constructionally possible, spans can be great especially with bridges, where distances of 1.5 km or more can be spanned whilst extensive cantilevers can also be constructed. However, in order that our buildings look stable and give confidence to the users the designer must go beyond simply ensuring that the building stands up. Figure 36 contrasts two buildings that are roughly the same height. One building appears stable whilst the other does not convey this impression because of the very small dimensions of its, otherwise, perfectly adequate structural supports.

This method of giving emphasis to the base of a building is a traditional way of presenting 'apparent' stability. Loads on the walls of the buildings increase towards the bottom and an early structural discovery was that walls needed to be thicker and stronger at the base than at the top. As more sophisticated forms of construction developed it often became less necessary, from a purely structural point of view, to build walls thicker, or in a material that could take greater loads, towards the base. Nevertheless the habit of giving the impression of stronger materials at the base continued for many years. Plate 24 shows the graduation in emphasis of jointing of the stone walls of the Banqueting House, Whitehall from the channelled joints in the basement forming a solid base to the building to the ashler work at

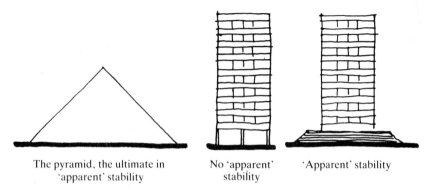

The pyramid, the ultimate in 'apparent' stability

No 'apparent' stability

'Apparent' stability

Figure 36 *'Apparent' stability.*

the top of the building. This gives the same impression—as does the pyramid—of greater stability at the base and lighter loads at the top. This principle persisted throughout the nineteenth century and well into the twentieth century. Often buildings were constructed with plinths that extended out beyond the face of the main building, an effect giving the impression of the foundations extending up above ground level.

Convenience

To be a fine piece of architecture a building must be convenient for its users, in other words it must 'work' from a planning point of view. The planning of buildings has been discussed in detail in Chapter 6.

Beauty

The oft-quoted statement that 'Beauty is in the eye of the beholder' is frequently used to dampen discussion on this topic. The appreciation of beauty must, nevertheless, be a subjective one. However, there are certain commonly held principles that determine visual beauty in building as much as there are those for music, poetry, prose, painting, or any other of the arts.

The factors which influence beauty in this case are composition, unity, balance, rhythm, proportion, scale, identity, manners, detail, colour, texture, pattern, and contrast.

Composition
Any schoolchild knows that a 'composition' requires a beginning, a

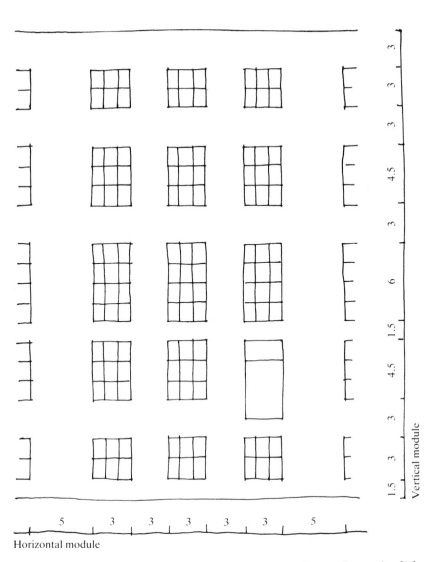

Vertical module

3
3
3
3
4.5
3
6
1.5
4.5
3
3
1.5

Horizontal module

5　3　3　3　3　3　5

Figure 37   Façade of Georgian house showing relationships of solid and void, which give rhythm and punctuation.

middle and an ending, or an introduction, a main body and a conclusion. So it is with buildings, exactly as a piece of written work must be broken down into paragraphs and sentences to enable the reader to pause, so too should a building be punctuated with vital elements. The Georgian designers were very skilled at this and their façades were punctuated with stops at the top and bottom generally in the form of square windows whilst string courses formed pauses in the rhythm of their composition of solid and void. Figure 37 shows a typical Georgian façade for a town house indicating this rhythm and punctuation.

One of the problems of many recent high-rise buildings is this lack of any definite punctuation especially at the top—so many buildings look as if they could easily have had several storeys more or less and that the termination was purely arbitrary (see Plate 29). Earlier high-rise buildings made use of cornices and arched openings to provide this termination and Plate 30 shows an example of this. A similar situation arises with long buildings. Traditional methods of end termination have been setting forward the last bay or bays and possibly raising them by one, or more, storeys; this acts as a positive terminal point for the eye which does not just drift off into the distance. Even modest two-storey Victorian streets often had a three storey building at the end—usually a public house—which acted as the punctuation stop for the terrace.

Not only does the eye need to be stopped at the end but it also needs to be drawn to the focal point of the building (often the entrance). This is usually fairly simple where the building is symmetrical but where the façade is asymmetrical a more conscious effort is often needed. For symmetrical façades the centre of attraction is usually located in the middle and, in the case of the entrance, is either set forward or recessed back to give emphasis. Furthermore, ornamentation is often

Plate 29   Local Authority Housing, Battersea, Greater London, 1970.

Plate 30   Bayard Building, New York, 1898 (Louis Sullivan). Photo courtesy of: Julian Feary architects.

Plate 31   State Library of New South Wales, Sydney, 1942 (New South Wales Government Architects). Photo courtesy of: New South Wales Government.

associated with this part of the building which acts additionally as an eye arrestor. Plate 31 shows an example of a building that has stops at either end and has a central block set forward to act as a focal point of the composition.

Unity

Any idea or conception for a building must be complete and not composed of scattered elements unrelated to one another. If this is the case defusion, rather than unity, exists. It is this unity in architecture that marks the difference between architectural composition and some haphazard arrangement of scattered architectural elements. To produce unity in architecture, as in all things, it is necessary to have some central or focal idea in the composition which should be clearly apparent and which should tend to dominate as in St Paul's Cathedral, London where the dome clearly dominates (see Plate 32). Alternatively, it is possible to have a number of similar elements of varying sizes which come together to form a dominant group as at the Palace of Westminster, London (see Plate 33). The

120

Plate 32   St Paul's Cathedral, Greater London, 1675–1710 (Sir Christopher Wren).

Plate 33   Palace of Westminster, Greater London, 1840–1860 (Sir Charles Barry).

unified theme of a building should not be confined to the exterior but should extend to the interior.

In this book, the virtue of Georgian designers has been indicated. These designers generally carried the unity of the external façade into the interior of the building through the use of similar elements such as columns and pilasters. However, they rarely carried any form of unity between façades unless two or more were very apparently visible. The eighteenth-century country houses did maintain unity between one façade and another, but this was very rare on the town houses which frequently had very unfortunate back views.

Balance

Buildings should present a restful appearance and in order to produce this the composition needs to be balanced.

Symmetrical buildings (see Figures 38 and 39) usually have their main entrance on the centre line, which means that the eye is drawn to this central focal point and the building balances about it. For asymmetrical buildings the problem is more difficult. Figure 40 shows a well-balanced asymmetrical composition whilst Figure 41 shows one that is unbalanced. From these sketches it can be seen that the balanced composition gives an air of repose missing from the unbalanced composition.

Proportion

One of the few aesthetic principles that can be analysed mathematically is that of proportion. Although the Ancient Greeks were masters at the design of elegant and finely proportioned buildings (see Plate 34) it was Vituvius in his ten books on Architecture (see Chapter 1) who first set out the principles of proportion.

As mentioned in the section on shape the eye is confused if it is not certain whether it is observing a square or a rectangle. The eye finds a square (that is a 1:1 proportion) pleasing, and it is also happy with a rectangle providing it is a definite rectangle finding the 5:3 proportion particularly pleasing.

The double square proportions 2:1 can again be confusing as the eye tries to divide this into two squares (see Figures 42 and 43). Once a rectangular proportion considerably exceeds 2:1 then the eye is content once again (see Figure 44). The eighteenth-century architects and pattern-book authors were very concerned with proportion, shapes and their relationship to one another. Figure 37 shows the make-up of proportions on the façade of a typical Georgian town house. Here the height of windows are clearly related to their widths

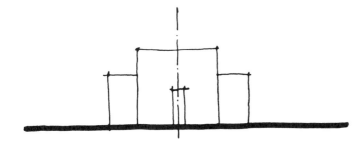

Figure 38   Balanced symmetrical building.

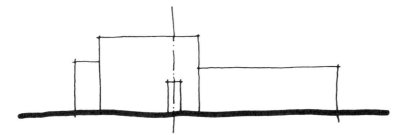

Figure 39   Balanced asymmetrical building.

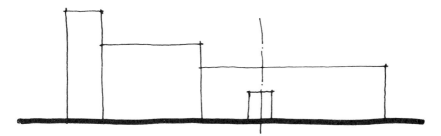

Figure 40   Unbalanced asymmetrical building.

Figure 41   Symmetrical building with duality.

Plate 34   Parthenon, Athens BC447–BC432 (Ictinus and Calli-crates). Photo courtesy of: Julian Feary architects.

and to the space in between with the square windows acting as a stop to the top and bottom of the façade.

Whilst concentrating on the appearance of windows and doors from an external viewpoint it is essential not to ignore the internal view of such components. Windows and doors are the principal components in which proportion manifests itself on a building's façade. However, other parts of a building need to be related one to another in a well-proportioned way. Examples of this are the relationship between wall and roof, or between different parts of a wall clad in differing materials.

Scale

One of the main criticisms levelled at many buildings built in the last few decades has been that they are 'inhuman'. What is usually meant is that they are 'inhuman in scale'—in other words they do not relate to the human being but more to the machine.

In the past—at least until the latter years of the nineteenth century —buildings were built entirely by men mainly using materials that originated directly from the soil—stone, clay to make bricks or tiles,

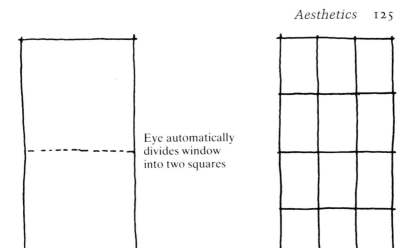

Eye automatically
divides window
into two squares

Figure 42 (left)   Double square window showing duality.

Figure 43 (right)   Duality resolved.

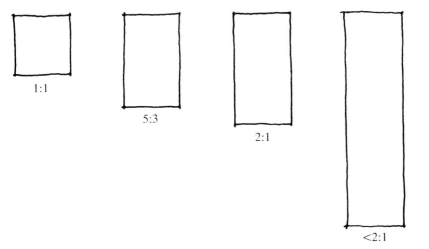

1:1

5:3

2:1

<2:1

Figure 44   Window proportions.

timber, thatch or palm leaves, sand, lime, cow dung and so on—and these were worked by man, hauled to the site perhaps with the help of animals and lifted into place possibly using simple lifting equipment aided occasionally by animals. The limitation was invariably the human body—brick sizes were determined by the width of a man's hand, their length being double this to facilitate bonding and their thickness was related to the weight that could be lifted by a man in his left hand whilst he held the trowel and mortar in his right hand. Brick sizes were eventually standardized (in the early seventeenth century in England) but they were based on this human factor. Certain roof tiles were formed over a man's thigh whilst even glass was blown into discs the maximum size of which was determined by the strength of a man's lungs. The height of buildings related to providing adequate headroom and doors were just high enough to permit a man to walk through without stooping and wide enough to enable him to carry something through in one hand (see Plate 35, which shows an eighteenth-century public house). Certain structures such as religious buildings and palaces were built much larger but even here human scale was maintained by the careful use of string courses, statues and other man-sized elements (see Plate 36).

With the advent of the Industrial Revolution materials started to be mass produced and man had mechanical aids to transport and lift his

Plate 35   Green Man Public House, Putney, Greater London dating from the eighteenth century.

Plate 36   Exeter Cathedral, Devon, c.1375.

materials and components. Gradually it became more economical to make these components larger and in factories where conditions were better controlled. These larger components could be transported to site by rail, water or road and latterly even by air. It is now possible to build entire buildings without man touching any of the materials, and this has naturally led to a 'machine scale' emerging into buildings and this, combined with the use of manufactured materials rather than organic ones, has resulted in much recent building being 'in-human'. This need not be the case, however, providing due regard is paid to scale as well as to the other design principles. It is important to remember that windows, doors and ornamentation are the traditional areas where human scale can best be expressed in buildings.

Identity

It is important that buildings are easily identifiable—over the years we have come to associate certain forms of buildings with specific building types and when we are confronted with a building where the use is known, but which looks like something else, we are confused and generally do not like the look of it. For example, if a school looks

127

Plate 37   Infil houses, Sydney, New South Wales, 1972 (Richard John Dinham). Photo courtesy of: New South Wales Government.

like a factory or if a block of flats more closely resembles an office block we can be unhappy; strangely, however, if the resemblance is that of a building type of the whimsical past we may not be so disturbed—for example, a block of public lavatories may look like a cottage or a shopping centre may be built in the style of a medieval barn. With those exceptions which really are a rejection of the real building type (such as the public lavatories and shopping centres) we are much more content with buildings that express their function in a familiar and easily recognizable way.

Thus, in parts of the world with regular precipitation we like our houses to have pitched roofs and everywhere we prefer our religious buildings to take on traditional forms. These are buildings with a well-established and familiar development but what of buildings of a 'new' type—factories, office blocks, airports; even these have de- veloped an identity over the years and as these buildings have tended to exploit the materials and techniques of the Industrial Revolution and subsequent years we are much happier to see the forms of these buildings and their materials reflect these developments.

128

Manners

As mentioned in Chapter 4 few buildings are erected in splendid isolation. Virtually every new building nowadays has to be grafted into an existing built environment. When the surroundings are architecturally of a high standard, concern is usually expressed by local authorities, amenity or other pressure groups that the new building 'blends in'—this is stating the obvious. All new buildings must blend into their surroundings respecting and reflecting their neighbours. This does not mean that new designs should be a pastiche of adjacent buildings but that the new building should respect and reflect the form, shapes, lines, proportions, scale, colour, texture, and pattern of its neighbours. This has been very successfully done, for example, in the two infil houses in a Sydney Terrace (see Plate 37).

In determining a suitable design it may, nevertheless, be possible to contrast the new building with the existing providing the basic principles of contrast are followed. A number of successful examples

Plate 38   Headquarters offices and bank, Strand, Greater London, 1978 (Frederick Gibberd, Coombes & Partners). Photo courtesy of: Frederick Gibberd Coombes and Partners.

Plate 39   Offices for building society, West Ealing, Greater London, 1979 (Purcell, Miller, Tritton & Partners).

of this approach have been carried out, for example at Coutt's Bank, Strand, London, where in the restoration of this early nineteenth-century Nash façade an incongruous Edwardian Baroque infil block has been replaced with a sympathetic glass entrance area (see Plate 38).

Occasionally the surroundings are of such an indifferent nature that it may be better to start afresh but this decision must be carefully considered in the light of possible future developments. This was the case where the infil office buildings shown in Plate 39 was provided for a building society in an indifferent London suburban street.

Detail

The importance of detail to external façades and internal spaces can never be under-estimated. Too many modern details, particularly those that occur on standard mass-produced products are not of a particularly high standard of design. The careful selection of products that go together to form the overall building must be done with aesthetics in mind. Many standard windows, doors and other products are simply badly proportioned and badly detailed. They may

130

serve functional requirements but they do not give that special element of delight which is necessary in architecture. In selecting products care should be taken to ensure that the proportions are good, that the relationship between one part and another is satisfactory, that the elements are to scale, and the colour, texture, and pattern of the product is satisfactory for the particular situation in which it is to be used. The detailing of such items as window heads, sub-sills, thresholds, hoods over doors, details at eaves, and the junctions between one material and another, or one component and another need to be carefully thought out to ensure the maximum benefit from choice between these materials is derived.

Many items that appear on modern buildings appear to have been left entirely up to the workmen executing the job. Such things as positioning of rainwater pipes, and outlets, soil pipes, television antennae, flues for heating appliances, air intake and outlet for air conditioning and other forced ventilation systems, waste pipes, positioning of electric meters and switchgear, location and detailing of rubbish collection points, dustbins, incinerators and so forth are often ignored by the design team and the lack of consideration of these elements, which can in fact play a significant part in the external appearances of buildings, is readily apparent in the finished product. All parts of the building façade and massing must be given the same detailed thought as is given to the overall concept.

Colour
Colour can make a positive contribution to the external and internal appearance of buildings.

Colour can be broken down into three components, namely: hue, greyness (or intensity) and weight (or value or tone). *Hue* is the property of redness, yellowness, blueness and so on and it is that that distinguishes one colour from another. There are three primary colours, namely red, blue, and yellow, and therefore there are three basic hues. It is, however, possible to make up any number of colours by mixing various hues. The British Standard on colour BS 5252: 1976 *Framework for Colour Co-ordination for Building Purposes* restricts itself to twelve hues, namely: red-purple, red, yellow-red (two variations), yellow, green-yellow, green, blue-green, blue, purple-blue, violet and purple and these can be arranged in a colour circle (see Figure 45). In addition, it identifies neutral, that is, lack of hue. *Greyness* (or intensity) is the estimated grey content in colours and the British Standard further divides colours into five groups, representing the various steps of diminishing greyness, namely: grey, nearly grey, grey/clear, nearly clear and clear. The *weight* (or value or

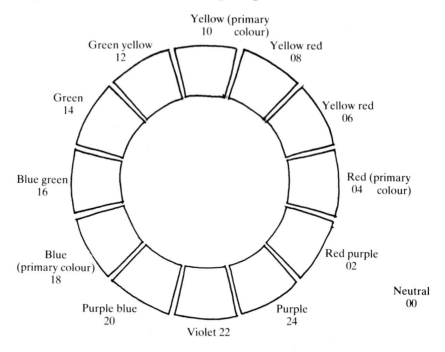

*Figure 45   Colour circle adapted from Oswald but using British
Standard colours.*

tone) of a colour is the amount of lightness or darkness contained in
the colour. A light colour in weight terms will reflect more light than
a dark colour although both may be of the same hue. Some hues are
lighter than others, for example yellow is lighter than blue.

By using these three components, hue, greyness and weight, it is
possible to describe any particular colour and thus avoid the confusion which occurs by referring to colours as peacock blue, venetian
red, and so on. It also ensures that where a specific colour is required
on a different material, such as paint for a wall, or on a fabric, or on a
ceramic tile, that a particular colour can be achieved without confusion or error. The British Standard three-part number—for example,
08B15 (yellow-red)—identifies hue (08), greyness (B) and weight (15);
this approximates a Munsell Reference of 10YR9.25/1 which is
another common method of describing colours.

Obviously the quality of the light in which a colour is viewed at any
particular time will affect the colour sensation that is received by the
viewer. The British Standard suggests that colour should always be

considered in good natural daylight which is desirable as far as definition of colour is concerned. However, in many instances, colours will never be seen in good natural daylight, whilst in others it may well be desirable to alter the type of light playing upon the colour in order to change the sensation of that colour.

Colours are further affected by the colours against which they are seen, and it is in this that full effects of colour can be exploited. There are two principal ways in which colours can be combined, namely harmony and contrast. Harmonious arrangements of colour occur when colours adjacent to one another on the colour circle (see Figure 45) are used. Generally speaking, when harmonious colours are used together, they can be in fairly equal quantities and of similar hue, greyness and weight. Contrast, on the other hand, occurs when colours that are opposite to one another on the colour circle are used together (for example, violet and yellow). Where contrasting colours are used one colour usually intensifies the other and draws the attention of the viewer to the dominant colour. Generally speaking, contrast in colour—as with contrast in any other aspect of design —should be based on the principle of one of the two contrasting elements dominating over the other in mass or area. Thus, when contrasting (for example) red and green, a large area of green should be used invariably with a small area of red or a large area of red with a small area of green. When this is done, it will be seen that the small area of contrasting colour will intensify the other colour.

Colours affect people in different ways and most people can be said to have a favourite colour as well as a colour that they dislike. It is often very difficult to find out what the reason is behind this tendency to favour one colour or dislike another but it is frequently a psychological one—for example, somebody who spent a fairly unhappy childhood in a room with a vivid blue colouring may well have a psychological dislike of blue, associating it with a rather unpleasant period in his or her life. Tests have shown that people with certain psychological disorders can benefit from changes in colour schemes, whilst for long-stay medical patients it has been shown that certain colours actually stimulate a more rapid medical recovery.

Colours also tend to go through stages of fashion, at one time green and cream were particularly fashionable colours, especially for kitchens or bathrooms. Other colours have undergone fashion from time to time, such as reds, browns and blues. Sometimes these are related to fashionable colours in clothing and in more recent years the pampas or greeny-beige colour for bathroom suites has been particularly popular.

Colours have other characteristics and can thus be considered to be cool or warm, and advancing or retreating. This is because the eye refocuses on different colours with the result that it can be said that the warm colours such as reds and yellows tend to advance towards you, while the cool colours such as blues and greens recede. This phenomena is also affected by the weight of the colour. Pale colours tend to recede, whereas strong colours tend to advance. This can, of course, be used to great effect in buildings—for example, in a very long corridor where it would be desirable to give the impression of foreshortening. Here an advancing colour could be used on the end walls and receding colours on the side walls. Where ceilings are high it is sometimes useful to use an advancing colour on the ceiling in order to give the visual effect of the ceiling being lower, whereas in the more common instances of low ceilings a receding pale colour would be chosen to emphasize the height of the space and also to reflect more light.

There are certain accepted colour responses, and these need to be borne in mind when selecting colours for particular parts or areas of a building. For example, blue tends to be soothing but an excess of deep blue can be depressing, and in addition blue is not a colour that should be used in large areas externally. Green has a similar effect as blue but should not be used externally where there are lots of natural greens such as trees, grass, fields etc. Yellow is bright and warm, being associated with the sun and is thus usually a very cheerful and stimulating colour; it can also be used to symbolize warning. Red is an exciting, warm colour, and it tends to be friendly, but it should not be used in large areas, unless in a pale form; red also constitutes danger. Purple can be used in small areas to signify richness, but should be avoided in large areas as it tends to be depressing and funereal. Neutral colours such as black, white, brown and grey can be extremely useful. However, black cannot really be used in large areas for practical purposes. White reflects a vast amount of light and therefore can produce a great deal of glare at certain times. Grey in large areas is very depressing especially under bleak northern skies. Browns are usually soothing and warm, especially when used in conjunction with reds, oranges and yellows.

Texture
Texture will always tend to modify colour, in that the same hue when used on a rough-textured surface will appear to be different from that seen when used on a smooth surface. Much texture is inherently contained in building materials—for example, stone, brick, timber and other natural building materials all tend to have a rough texture of varying degrees whilst manufactured materials such as steel, glass

and plastic tend to have a smooth texture unless special provisions are made in the manufacturing process in order to attain a rough surface. One of the problems of texture produced during the manufacturing stage is that it tends to be of a very even nature which may be desirable in certain instances, but (for example) reconstructed and artificial stones made in the same mould will have a uniformity of texture that will not be as pleasing as the texture that is obtained from natural building stones worked by hand, where there will be a unique texture for each particular stone. Texture, like colour, is affected by the way in which light falls upon it and this can be exploited extensively both through the skilful use of natural sunlight and artificial light. Light falling at an acute angle on to a textured surface will emphasize the texture much more so than the light that is normal to that surface. Texture is also affected by distance, and something that appears quite rough close at hand may well appear to be very smooth when viewed from a distance. This is an important consideration in the design of tall buildings where, for example, a rough texture is required at the top of the building where it will have to be considerably rougher than that required at the bottom of the building if it is to give the same impression. Textures can be contrasted in the same way as colour and basically the same principle applies, in that there should be a large area of one particular texture and small area of contrasting texture in order to maximize the effect.

Pattern .

The arrangement of various elements on the facade of a building can produce a pattern. On most buildings this pattern will be a composition of squares or rectangles triangles or semi-circles and these will usually be made up in a regular pattern.

Reference should be made to those sections earlier in this chapter dealing with line and proportion, indicating the effect that various components making up the pattern will have on the visual appearance of the building. Smaller patterned areas on buildings can be incorporated by carefully arranging the bonding of, for example, brick or tiles and possibly even by changing colour. The Victorians were masters at this particular effect and very interesting patterns were often achieved on their buildings with the use of different coloured bricks which formed horizontal bands, chequerboard or herring-bone patterns. The arrangement of transomes, mullions and glazing bars and so on on windows all contribute to pattern and all too often this pattern is destroyed when replacement windows are incorporated.

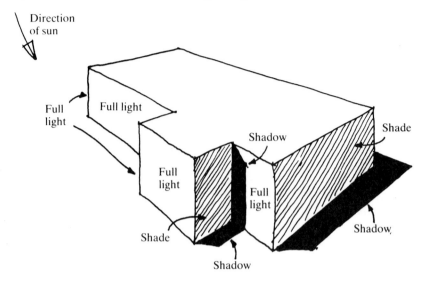

Figure 46   Shade and shadow.

Shade and shadow

The external appearance of buildings is affected by the light in which the building is viewed. Under normal circumstances the primary source of light during daytime is the sun, and this light will vary depending upon time of day and period of the year as well as from one part of the world to another, depending on such factors as the aspect of the particular facade, the latitude, the cloud cover, and atmospheric conditions prevailing at that particular point. The appearance of colours, textures and patterns will be affected greatly by the intensity of light falling upon them and whether or not these particular surfaces are in shade or in shadow. Shadow occurs when a particular element prevents sunlight from reaching that surface by the inter-position of some other particular element, whilst shade is where the light does not actually strike that surface directly (see Figure 46).

In those parts of the world where sunlight can be relied upon, very interesting effects on the façade of a building can be created, by means of overhanging roofs, deep reveals on windows, balconies, window boxes, canopies, and so on making ever-changing patterns of light, shade and shadow on the façade of buildings and thus giving an interesting changing pattern. In more northern countries, however, sunshine cannot generally be relied upon, and where buildings have been designed, especially in heavily textured and sculptured concrete, these have not proved to be successful during the part of the year when strong sunlight does not reach their surfaces. Here pattern has often resulted from staining of rain running down the façade, rather than from the intense light of the sun.

At night time, light is usually from artificial sources because only on very rare occasions is the light of the moon strong enough to produce shadow and shade. Thus artificial lighting will invariably be of a different colour and from a different source and direction to that of natural sunlight. This must be borne in mind together with the actual arrangement of the lighting which will greatly affect the appearance of the building, for example, in floodlights where the light source comes from below, this will reverse the shade and shadow, compared to that when the light source is the sun from above.

Contrast

Contrast has been mentioned already in various parts of this chapter, especially relating to colour and to texture. Contrast is an essential element in the design of buildings, in the same way as it is in our everyday life, and whilst it is most common to have contrast in buildings in colour or texture, it is also possible to contrast form, proportions, line, shape, solid and void, and any of the other elements which contribute towards the visual quality of a building. Wherever contrast is used one of the contrasting elements must always dominate in mass or shape, or size, over the other element. If this is not done, the eye will not know upon which element it should rest with the result that there will be confusion.

The fourth dimension

It would not be appropriate to close the chapter on aesthetics without considering the fourth dimension (or time) as a factor of design of buildings. Virtually all buildings have a very long life, on average at least 100 years. During this time, the buildings will change, the materials will weather, and age, and depending on the quality of maintenance on the building, it will either deteriorate or develop a charm which only age can give. The design team thus needs to carefully consider what the building will look like in (say) 20 years time, given different degrees of maintenance. If as much future maintenance as possible can be eliminated at the original design stage, the building will be far more successful both aesthetically and economically in the long run. However, the effect of weather and time must not be forgotten; the constant battering by rain and wind, the bleaching of the sun and the effects of snow and frost on various materials must be considered and the good design team will exploit these by ensuring that this weathering process will enhance the appearance of the building and not detract from it.

Another aspect of time needs considering, and this is the effect of grandiose schemes on a particular area, and one example is particularly worth citing. In the 1950s the planners of Edinburgh decided that in order to alleviate the traffic congestion in Princes Street, Edinburgh's principal and famous shopping street, they would require that all new buildings in that street should be provided with an upper level walkway, so that eventually the shops and the pedestrians could be moved to first floors. Over the following years, new buildings in Edinburgh's Princes Street, were built to comply with these requirements. However, at no point is there today a continuous walkway, nor did the problem of crossing the important North–South streets such as Castle Street and Hanover Street appear to receive full consideration. In 1984 this scheme was abandoned. There are now a number of short upper-level walkways, with provision for shops, pedestrians still jostle with traffic at street level and the entire scheme has been beaten by time. The empty upper-floor showrooms with wide balconies which were to be footpaths enjoy, for the most part, superb views over Princess Street Gardens, to the castle and to Arthur's Seat in the background and have potential for conversion into restaurants with the proposed walkways glazed to protect the diners against the cold climate.

It is unlikely that such grandiose schemes will be put forward in the near future. However, the design team must always be on their guard against schemes that are of such a profound nature that they will affect the appearance of buildings and streets for years to come.

Conclusion

The spirit of our age demands that the appearance of buildings should be a true reflection of the solution of all the problems posed by planning, climatic, site, technical, legal, and economic constraints. A good solution to these constraints will determine the choices relating to stability and convenience. They will also determine many of the principles involved in the determination of beauty—composition, unity, balance, form, shape, line, proportion, scale, identity, manners, detail, colour, texture, shade and shadow, pattern, contrasts, and time. However, the building that gives pure delight will be the one that solves all of these problems to produce a stable, convenient and beautiful result.

References

Bloomer, C. M. *Principles of Visual Perception* (Van Nostrand Reinhold: New York, 1976).

British Standards Institute BS5252: 1976 *Framework for Colour Co-ordination for Building Purposes* (BSI: London, 1976).

Krier, R. *Elements of Architecture* (Academy: London, 1984).

Scruton, R. *The Aesthetics of Architecture* (Methuen: London, 1979).

Smithies, K. W. *Principles of Design in Architecture* (Van Nostrand Reinhold: New York, 1981).

8

Special problems

Introduction

The design team is frequently confronted with special problems when designing buildings or groups of buildings. Whilst it is not possible to highlight all of these in a book of this nature there are three specific types of problems that are commonly encountered nowadays. These are:

1 extensions to existing buildings;
2 rehabilitation and conservation; and
3 making provisions for disabled persons.

In all cases the normal design process of brief, analysis, synthesis, implementation, and feedback will need to be followed. In virtually all cases the same constraints to the designs will apply—climate, site, technical, economic, legal, planning and aesthetic. The order in which these constraints may have to be considered may vary but none can be ignored.

Extensions to existing buildings

The first constraint that must be considered before deciding whether to extend an existing building is the legal one.

In Britain certain domestic buildings can be extended by a modest amount without obtaining planning permission. There are rigid requirements relating to this which should be checked to ensure that the proposals do constitute a permitted development before proceeding.

In addition to obtaining planning permission there may be other legal requirements that have to be complied with before any extension work can be carried out. Such things as restrictive covenants may apply to certain properties, the building may be listed, or it may be in a conservation area. There may be restrictions on extensions for particular types of buildings. Local planning authorities may, in addition, not wish to have some types of buildings extended, thereby providing more floor space for a particular use, which they may feel is detrimental to a particular part of the area under their jurisdiction. For example, at certain times over the last couple of decades in London there have been restrictions on extensions to office buildings. It is necessary to obtain all necessary approvals for extensions as if building from scratch while in some cases the restrictions are likely to be even more onerous with regard to extension work.

Adjoining owners should always be contacted as early as possible and kept in the picture as to what is proposed to be done on the land that is going to be covered by the extension. In most instances, planning authorities carry out this operation, but in the interests of good neighbourliness it is wise to approach the adjoining owners during the brief stage and if possible discuss proposals with them. Adjoining owners will usually be anxious if there is any likelihood that they will loose privacy, or light, or sunshine in any part of their building or the surrounding ground which they use as an amenity.

Economic constraints are often more important for extensions than for new buildings. In many cases, especially in domestic work it will not be possible to recoup the cost of the extension in the short term whilst even in the long term any financial return to the property owner may only accrue due to inflation. This is particularly the case where the property being extended forms part of a development of properties similar in size and design. Extensions are invariably purpose-built and are not necessarily exactly what a prospective purchaser may require. The possibility thus exists that other similar properties that are on the market at the same time will be purchased in preference because of the lower asking price.

When it comes to extending premises other than domestic then consideration must be given to the convenience of carrying out the extension and whether it may be better for the client to consider selling his interest in that particular property and moving to another site or to a larger building. Certain building uses must remain in their present situation. It would not be at all possible to relocate certain transportation buildings or commercial or industrial premises which are totally dependent upon their being located in the particular position that they occupy.

Having decided at the analysis stage that an extension is going to be feasible for a particular building project, the synthesis stage will pose specific problems. The first of these will be whether the extension

Plate 40   Extension to the Natural History Museum, Kensington, Greater London, 1976 (Prickheard & Partners).

should be built in a style that matches or contrasts with the existing building. Plates 40 and 41 show two different extensions to buildings. Plate 40 is an extension carried out in the contrasting style, whilst Plate 41 is an extension carried out in the style similar to that of the existing building. When the design team decides to use a contrasting style the principles of contrast covered in Chapter 7 should be followed. One of the elements should always exceed the other in mass sufficiently to avoid duality. In most cases this means that either the extension must be considerably smaller than that of the existing building or the extension must be considerably larger. Where an extension is going to be of roughly the same bulk as that of the existing building then it is generally wiser to consider extending in the existing style. When the decision has finally been made as to which style to use, then certain other principles should be followed.

For an extension to be carried out in a style that matches that of the existing building it is necessary to consider what new materials can be purchased that will give the same appearance and the same feel as those employed on the existing building. Virtually all modern day materials are machine made and mass produced. These do not necessarily blend in satifactorily with the hand-made materials from a previous age. It may therefore be necessary to obtain second-hand

142

Plate 41   Extension to Gower Street façade, University College, Greater London, 1985 (Casson Conder & Partners).

materials or to search for manufacturers who still use traditional processes. Hand-made and second-hand materials are often considerably more expensive than their machine-made modern counterparts. It is important that the materials should be of the same manufactured method as those employed in the original building otherwise there is little or no chance that as the building starts to weather the extension will blend in with the existing building to any great degree.

It is then necessary to go about the design of the exterior of the building in a way that will enable the new part to blend in with the old. Proportions for the windows and doors and the spaces between these and such elements as string courses, cornices and roof details should be continued through in such a way that the new building fully matches the existing. Many old buildings are very elaborately ornamented and this produces problems that can sometimes be overcome by using new materials. (For example, in certain instances, glass re-inforced plastic or reconstructed stone can be used to produce ornament). Unfortunately glass re-inforced plastic will not weather like plastered brickwork and reconstructed stone will not weather in the same way as natural stone.) Nevertheless, where the materials are

143

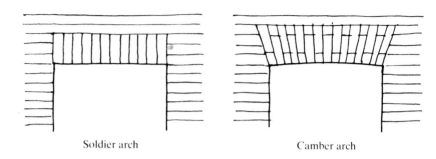

Soldier arch   Camber arch

Figure 47   Soldier and camber arches.

used high up on a building they may be acceptable.

When matching windows, doors and other elements the detail of the original must be followed. The frames should be set back in reveals, or finished flush with the outside walls as on the existing façade. If windows are not positioned on the same plane in relation to the wall face, no matter how good a replica they are they will not look the same. Not only must the proportions and details of the element be the same but also the sizes of various members that make up that element. For a window this means that sashes and glazing bars, jambs, heads, and sills, together with sub-sill and the detail of the support of the wall at the head of the window must match the existing examples. Soldier arches are not a suitable substitute for brick camber arches (see Figure 47). Figure 48 shows a method of keeping the same proportion within the window whilst changing its overall size.

Other details that must match are those at eaves, including gutters, and parapets, string courses and at the base of walls. On many old buildings chimneys are an essential element of the design and will need to be incorporated in the extension where they can provide flues for boilers or ventilation shafts.

Extensions in contrasting styles pose different problems for the design team. Once a contrasting style has been decided upon it is necessary to ensure that this style is, in fact, a contrasting style and not some *ad hoc* variance of the existing building which neither compliments the existing building nor contrasts with it. The appearance of the existing building must be looked at fully at the analysis stage. Most older buildings, that is buildings built before the 1930s, consisted predominantly of solid, with a small amount of void in the

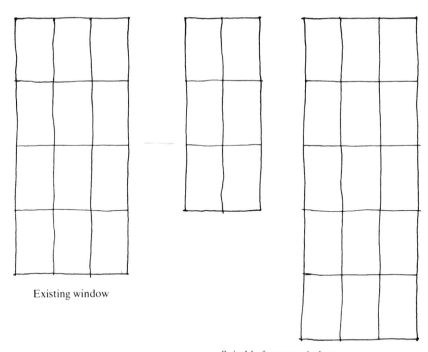

Existing window

Suitable for new windows

Figure 48   Method of maintaining the same proportion within a window whilst changing its overall size.

form of windows and doors. In most cases the roof was a dominant element of the building, whilst in some cases the roof dominated over the walls. Chimneys were an important part of buildings even in warmer countries simply because an open fire or range was the predominant means of cooking and boilers using solid fuel were the principal means of producing hot water. Thus most older buildings consist mainly of some form of wall surface punctured by a relatively small number of fairly small window openings. The wall is capped with a roof whose skyline is broken by chimneys.

To achieve an extension in a contrasting style one solution is to reverse the relationship between solid and void so that if in the existing building, for example, there is a relationship of three parts solid to one part void it may be felt that in the extension one part solid to three parts void may well prove a suitable contrasting solution. The materials for the wall surface may also be treated as a contrasting

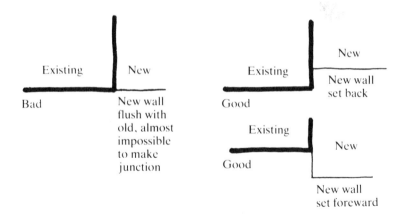

Figure 49   Wall junction plans.

material, hence if the existing building is rendered, a good-quality facing brick may be chosen for the extension. On the other hand render may be used where the original building is in facing brick or stone. Alternatively, some other form of cladding may be chosen for the extension such as weatherboarding, tile hanging or marble. These can be selected to provide a contrast in colour or texture, always remembering (of course) the principles of contrast mentioned earlier. Even when constructing buildings in contrasting style it is necessary to maintain the scale and the proportions of the existing building.

With a contrasting style it is not necessary to continue details through in the way that they are in the original building. However, floor levels and other horizontal elements may be marked in the way that string courses and ornamentations have marked the adjoining building, but possibly in a simpler way.

Whether the decision is made to use a style that blends, or one that contrasts, with the existing building, then it is still essential that certain key junctions are considered very carefully. For example, walls should be set back in junctions rather than lining up (see Figure 49) whilst with roofs, it is usually better to tuck an extension roof underneath the existing eaves rather than to try and continue the roof line down (see Figure 50).

Wherever possible flat roofs should be avoided for extensions to buildings which already have a pitched roof. Where a flat roof is inevitable on an extension then special care must be taken with its junction with the main building. It is much more desirable if the flat

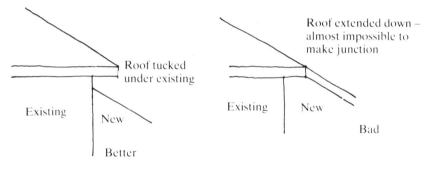

Figure 50 Roof junction elevations.

roof tucks under the main roof and eaves rather than running into the roof, which usually results in a rather ugly junction. The principal weakness of a flat roof from an aesthetic point of view is its termination with the walls. As has been mentioned earlier in Chapter 7 a building requires a definite stop so that the eye is arrested at the top of the building and does not just fade off into the distance. The traditional pitched roof provides a very satisfactory cap to most buildings. However, with a flat roof the need for a consciously designed stop is of paramount importance. One of the ways of solving the problem is to extend the wall upwards to form a parapet and where this is done proper consideration must be given to the relationship between the top of the windows of the top most floor and the underside of the coping or other finish on the parapet. Reference back to the façade of the Georgian building shown in Figure 37 indicates just how important this particular detail and proportion was to Georgian builders.

On many city sites it is often desirable to extend the building upwards. On older buildings, especially those built before the early part of the twentieth century, there are often difficulties of loading because the foundations were frequently very poor by present-day standards. Nevertheless, in some cases it is constructionally feasible to extend the building upwards and even when foundations are inadequate it is possible to underpin existing foundations, though this is obviously expensive. Many early framed buildings, (that is, those using steel and concrete) were over-designed by present-day standards, and so after careful consideration by the structural engineer it may prove possible to add an extra storey or two to these buildings without any detriment to the structure. In virtually all cases, local planning authorities will be concerned about buildings that are to be extended upwards, and may have some guidance to offer the design team in order to attain a certain uniformity, where upward extensions are fairly commonplace. In recent years in Britain the addition of mansard storeys have proved popular even to the extent that some writers have coined the phrase 'mansarditis' implying that providing you put a mansard roof on the building the planning authority will be happy with the completed solution.

Generally the same principles apply to the design of extensions upwards on buildings as to extensions outwards. However, the constructional problems are invariably much greater and it is usually necessary to pay particular attention to access and egress including means of escape provisions. Extensions upwards require lighting in the form of windows or roof lights, and again the principle must be observed of respecting or contrasting the extension with that of the existing building. Figures 51 and 52 show two examples of different ways of adding an additional storey to a terraced house of late eighteenth- early nineteenth-century in London.

In too many cases, attics of houses have been converted with totally inappropriate forms of windows. Dormer windows that are far too large and bear little or no relationship to the existing window proportions, and/or dormers that have been extended to provide additional head height in the upstairs converted rooms and provide a very extensive amount of solid external walling are most unpleasing aesthetically. Dormer windows were originally inserted in roofs to provide light and ventilation, not head room, and the fact that in most parts of the world the cheeks were solid was only for purposes of construction. The flat-roofed dormer is particularly inappropriate to most building types. A quick look around the existing buildings that had rooms in their attic in any region would show the dormer windows are either roofed with hips, gables, segmental, or eyebrow-type roofs. In some places a simple pitched, or pent, roof running from the ridge was brought down over the dormers. Various traditional forms of dormer windows are shown in Figure 53 and where dormers are to be used the most appropriate type should be chosen for the particular locality.

When it comes to planning extensions there are invariably particular problems of access. It is usually necessary to break through existing walls in order to provide access to lateral extensions, and often changes of level result. Safety considerations tend to control the minimum number of steps permissible as well as the slopes of ramps, and these have to be taken into consideration where these changes of level occur. It is often necessary to provide new corridors through the

Figure 51 Extension upwards in style of existing building: (a) section; (b) elevation.

Figure 52 Extension upwards in contrasting style: (a) section; (b) elevation.

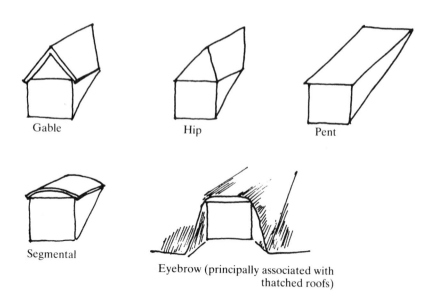

Gable   Hip   Pent

Segmental

Eyebrow (principally associated with
thatched roofs)

Figure 53   Various types of dormer windows commonly found in Britain.

existing buildings to provide access to the new extension. Care must be taken lighting these and in providing necessary fire protection as well as ensuring that internal details are not destroyed by the new partitions. Where extensions occur upwards additional staircases will have to be provided. Some staircases are much easier to extend upwards than others. For example, the dog-leg staircase usually permits easy upwards extension whilst occupying a minimum of floor area as shown in Figure 54 which also shows how difficult it is to extend a straight flight staircase upwards. Here quite a large amount of floor area is wasted on the existing upper floor in order to get access around to the foot of the next flight of stairs. This point about stair design is worth remembering when building new small domestic buildings which are capable of being extended upwards by incorporating (wherever possible) the dog-leg type of staircase, as it makes the whole building task much easier if owners decided to extend their buildings.

Sometimes the additional floor can result in the building becoming classified in a different category as far as building regulations are

Rehabilitation and conservation

If the 1950s and the 1960s were the high-rise years, the 1970s and the 1980s must surely be considered the rehabilitation and conservation years. At the time this was a welcome relief to many but now there must be a real conviction that this is the right action before conserving buildings that appear to have come to the end of their useful life. There are many questions that must be answered. Why is it that we have become so concerned with conservation and rehabilitation of buildings? Has the pendulum swung too far away from redevelopment and new building? Are we in danger in conserving at any cost? Have any buildings been preserved beyond their natural life span simply because we have lacked the confidence of building anything which is going to be better?

Throughout the world there must be very many buildings that really should not be conserved, but which at the moment are susceptible to the fashion of conservation. That is not to say that conservation of very good quality buildings should not be carried out—of course it should but it is of vital importance that there is selection and that we only conserve the best of our historic buildings and groups of buildings. Those buildings that are not of a high standard and have come to the end of their life should be replaced with fine examples of new buildings reflecting the knowledge, technology, skills and requirements of the present day. At the present time, there is a lack of confidence in our ability as designers and builders, and a lack of confidence politically and socially in a way that has rarely been seen in the past. In building this is reflected not only in the amount of conservation and rehabilitation work that is going on, simply because there is concern that what will be put in its place will be worse, or at least not appreciably better, than that which exists. In addition when new buildings are being constructed there is now a tendency to revert to old styles. Buildings in mock vernacular, mock Tudor, mock Georgian, mock Regency, mock colonial, mock Victorian, mock Edwardian, even sometimes mock interwar are becoming more and more commonplace. The way has been lost and certainly the clear-sighted confidence of the designers of the international style is gone. There are some architects who are pointing the way with fine contemporary buildings as we have seen in Chapter 1: architects like Norman Foster, James Stirling and Richard Rogers in Britain, John Portman in the USA, and John Andrews in Australia.

Why should buildings be conserved? It has become so commonplace in recent years to conserve that many people have stopped asking themselves the simple question 'Why conserve?' However, it is certainly possible to justify conservation on historical grounds. We need to know about our history in order to understand the present and to be able to see towards the future. Throughout history buildings have been very closely linked with the social development of a country and its society, and it is thus impossible to appreciate how society developed without our built heritage. In addition, architecture is an art, the mother of all arts, but it is the one art that takes up an awful lot of space. No one would contemplate destroying a Rembrandt, a Constable, or a Picasso, even if he did not particularly like it. But paintings and sculpture can be stored in vaults and basements. The texts of literature and music can be filed away or be microfilmed, if at any particular point of time they are out of favour. Even the original manuscripts or scores, if they are available, do not take up a very great amount of space. Buildings, unfortunately, are different. They do take up space, and often that space is very valuable. Many of our most interesting old buildings are located in urban centres in the historic core of our towns and cities, which is where land is at its most valuable. Often these older buildings do not maximize the use of the site in the way that modern buildings would. However, they may still be art and are essential candidates for conservation.

In addition, nowadays there is a much greater awareness of the architectural heritage in every country. This has been brought about by increasing communications. Before World War II very few people other than architects ever studied the history of architecture, but now it is a much more common subject for study. There are many scholarly works available on the topic, whilst the many excellent television programmes on various aspects of the built environment have proved to be very popular and have provoked a much greater interest in architecture. In addition to this there is a much greater number of people travelling in their own country and abroad. During these tours or holidays people often make a point of visiting historic buildings and historic places.

However, it is necessary to set against these pro-conservation arguments those of the anti-conservationists, the most common of which is that conservation inhibits progress and change, and as we mentioned earlier in this chapter this is certainly the case in many situations. It is worth remembering that had the conservationists been as active in the past as they are today, many of the buildings and places that we are trying hard to conserve would never have been built in the first place. In London we would have a rather indifferent Norman cathedral at the top of Ludgate Hill instead of Wren's St Pauls, whilst on Bennelong Point, Sydney, a preserved tram shed would grace the view rather than the fine Opera House. In Paris there would be a maze of minor streets and mean buildings where the boulevards and avenues now cut through the city providing the vistas and all that we associate with that capital.

It has already been mentioned that buildings occupy sites, which are often very expensive, and that the buildings do not necessarily maximize the land available. If a building sitting in such a place is to be conserved then distortion easily occurs in the market situation. The owner of that building is required to operate at a lower degree of profitability for the sake of conserving his building. As the general public are going to profit by this conservation through being able to appreciate the building, or by being able to profit by the arrival of many visitors to view this building, then it would perhaps be realistic to assume that the reduction in profit to the owner of the building that has to be conserved should be borne by the public at large—in other words by the tax payer rather than the individual building owner. This, of course, opens up a veritable hive of controversy but, nevertheless, it needs to be borne in mind when considering whether the building should be conserved or not.

Often the most vocal people, as far as conservation is concerned, will not be the people who will be the final users of the conserved building. In many cases the users of the conserved building will be the less fortunate members of society who may have to suffer from living, working, being educated, or being looked after, when they are sick in buildings which may be very fine architecturally but may not suit the modern-day requirements. A case in point might be a Victorian hospital that does not match up to the needs of the late twentieth century, but is a fine building on a commanding site and where it has been decided, perhaps because of pressure groups, to retain that building rather than replace it with a modern one. There is a very good chance that this hospital will be located in an inner urban area and that it will be the main hospital for people living nearby who could well be rather disadvantaged. These residents will have had little or no say at all in whether the building should be conserved, or whether it should be torn down and replaced with a new efficient modern building perhaps located on a more convenient situation.

A hospital is perhaps a good point to concentrate on as far as conservation is concerned. Most people associate hospitals with high technology and with the latest in equipment and drugs. When admitted to hospital the best treatment and the latest equipment is expected. The latest facilities are usually located in a new building. The latest facilities and equipment would normally be expected to attract the best medical staff and most people would probably prefer to be admitted to the modern hospital rather than to an old hospital. This may not always be the case, as there must be countless old buildings in most countries that are in hospital use, have an excellent staff, and are very well equipped indeed. However, the high technology of present-day medical science is associated with 'high-tech' buildings in most peoples' minds.

Housing reacts remarkably easily to rehabilitation in most cases, even though changing life-styles and changing social needs have had a very big impact on house design over the last 100 years or so. Despite this it is often relatively easy to rehabilitate an old house to make it suitable either for a single family unit or for several flats which meet present-day requirements. Certain factors, which we take for granted in modern buildings, will have to be sacrificed in older ones that have been rehabilitated. For example, thermal and sound insulation standards may not be able to be to quite the same level as in a purpose-built building. Nor indeed could the maximization of solar gain form an essential part of the design as windows are usually restricted in size whilst their positions do not always respect the best aspect. It may well be that the principal rooms will end up facing north in the northern hemisphere in rehabilitated buildings.

There is often a problem with subsequent maintenance and repair of rehabilitated buildings. It is not sufficient to simply calculate the initial cost of rehabilitation versus new buildings, where—in most cases—it will be found that the rehabilitation will work out more economical. Figures of 15 to 20 per cent have been quoted for this, but of course this does not apply in every case, and in almost all cases rehabilitated work will have higher on-going maintenance demand than does new work. It is, perhaps, when this maintenance demand reaches a peak—perhaps some 15 years after the original rehabilitation—that people will come to realise they did not always get quite such a bargain that they thought they would get.

Older residential property usually contains much greater amounts of external paintwork, both on plaster and wood than is the case in new buildings and this is extremely expensive to maintain nowadays. The delightful early nineteenth-century fully rendered fronts of the larger London town houses require repainting every three or four years in order to keep up their pristine appearance which is expensive both of time and money, especially when one also considers the inevitable price of scaffolding that must be associated with work to these buildings. When older houses are converted into flats, problems arise with sound transmission as insulation can never be as effective as in new building work. Single-family dwellings usually had timber floors and did not have any sound insulation and whilst it is possible to upgrade these to a reasonable extent this still provides little sound resistance to modern stereo equipment. Other problems such as responsibility for communal spaces—not only externally but also internally—can result in difficulty with regard to rehabilitated and converted residential property.

Expansion of town centres, especially in the suburbs and in the country areas pose other problems when there are extensive conservation and rehabilitation policies especially with regard to shops. In the principal shopping streets of older town centres the shopping units are often small and originally contained residential accommodation above. These groups of buildings have usually been built over a fairly long period of time and have been subject to gradual replacement and renewal, with occasionally two or three shops being redeveloped together. This means that most of our town centres comprise narrow-fronted buildings without adequate service access fronting onto a street which often carries heavy traffic, both pedestrian and vehicular. Few high streets are level between one shop and another. This poses great problems when the design group wish to convert several of the shops to provide one large shopping floor area—to suit present day requirements—whilst at the same time attempting to preserve the façade. The large multiple stores of today therefore often abandon the conserved shopping areas in the centre. Instead they choose to build large, almost warehouse-type, shopping developments on the edges of towns with easy vehicular access for both delivery of goods and their customers providing ample car parking and large single level shopping facilities. These superstores, or hyperstores, attract the more affluent people in society, leaving the town centres to cater for the less mobile poor. In the centres small individually owned shops are often left with vacant space above them as the owners no longer tend to live above the shops. Gradually the town centres die, both economically and physically.

With other buildings, the finding of a use for them once they are conserved poses problems. Any community can only support a very limited number of museums and many conserved buildings are suited to little else. It takes great imagination, skill and money to convert many conserved buildings into uses that are both practical and economical for today's requirements. Nevertheless there have been numerous, very successful, examples of warehouses being converted into flats, churches being converted into community centres and flats, market halls being converted into small shopping arcades, churches into theatres, bars and restaurants, railway stations into professional offices. But there are many other fine buildings that should be conserved but where there is a lack of suitable use to which the building can be put. Thus it must be seriously questioned as to whether in those cases the conservation of these buildings really is a practical answer.

Needs of disabled persons in buildings

Over the last few years, designers have become much more conscious of the needs of disabled persons when designing their buildings. In Britain 1981 was the Year of the Disabled and attention was drawn during that year to the particular problems which disabled persons have in using buildings. Not only must the design team consider people who are wheelchair-bound, but it must also make provision for people who have general difficulty in moving and also for those with sight and hearing difficulties. In Britain legislation has been introduced which gives a certain amount of statutory strength to the actual provision of specific requirements within buildings. It is important at the outset to understand the difference between the ambulant, semi-ambulant and the wheelchair-bound as each of these particular groups of people have different requirements with regard to the use of a building.

The term 'ambulant' covers ambulant elderly people because most designs are built in a way that enables healthy ambulant people to use all of the facilities. However, elderly people who move more slowly, who can find stairs a trial, and who have greater difficulty in reaching for things, need special provisions made for them, especially in the home. For the most part, elderly ambulant people prefer to live on a single level, either in a bungalow or a flat. Where they do live in two-storey residences, it is particularly desirable that downstairs toilet and washing facilities should be provided in addition to the normal facilities upstairs. It is also good if provision can be made for the ambulant elderly to be able to sleep downstairs in two-storey houses on odd occasions if this becomes necessary.

However, it is the needs of the semi-ambulant and the wheelchair-bound that provide the greatest challenge in the design of buildings. The semi-ambulant can be described as people who walk with some form of assistance either by means of walking sticks or a walking frame. People who use walking aids of this type generally find stairs easier to cope with than ramps, although very shallow ramps, perhaps 1 in 20, are capable of being used by people using walking aids. However, if these ramps are external they can become treacherous even at pitches as shallow as 1 in 20 during frosty and sometimes even just wet weather.

For wheelchair-bound people the problems become much more

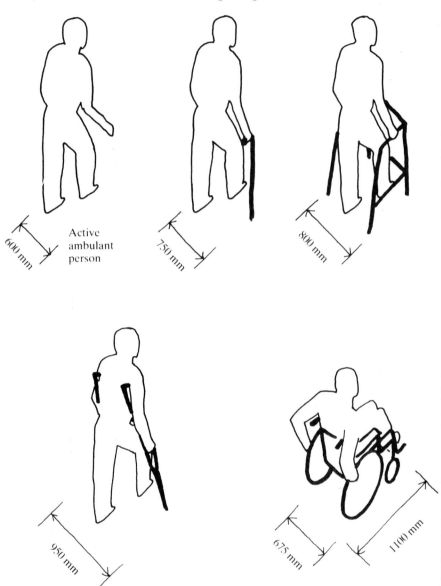

Active
ambulant
person

600 mm

750 mm

800 mm

950 mm

675 mm

1100 mm

Figure 55   Extra spatial requirement of disabled persons.

acute. It is impossible to use a wheelchair on stairs and even a very small change in level can be difficult to negotiate. In addition to this, wheelchairs take up space and generally require passageways and doorways to be wider than would normally be the case. Figure 55 indicates these extra special requirements. Ramps become essential for changing levels for wheelchair-bound persons and here minimum pitches are recommended, both for wheelchair-bound persons who are assisted and for those who propel themselves. Doors cause problems for persons in wheelchairs, especially those on spring hinges or with other automatic closing devices. Sliding doors generally are easier for disabled persons to operate and consideration should be given to eliminating doors altogether, where this is possible, especially in homes for disabled persons (for example, between the kitchen and the living room). Relaxations to regulations may be sought so that the sole bathroom/wc in a disabled persons home may open directly off the bedroom thus eliminating the need to pass through two doors between bedroom and bathroom. The mounting height of hardware on doors needs to be carefully considered so that somebody in a wheelchair can easily reach this to operate the door, whilst in public spaces vision panels need to be considerably lower than they would be on ordinary doors, preferably narrow vision panels extending virtually the full height of the door, which incidentally tend to look better than square vision panels placed near the top of the door. With people in wheelchairs more space is required in bedrooms to enable the transfer from wheelchair to bed to take place. In addition to this, extra space must be provided in the bathroom and toilet to enable the transfer from wheelchair to bath and WC pan.

There are a number of specific points that need to be considered when designing for wheelchair-bound people.

1   Access to buildings, wherever possible, should be covered from the point of exit from transport, whether this is ambulance or private car. Disabled persons, indeed all elderly persons, tend to move at a much slower rate than do active younger people, and therefore during inclement weather, they are likely to get wetter covering the same distance, or whilst doing similar tasks such as alighting from motor cars and locking same. Car ports are generally better than garages for this purpose as there is one less door for the disabled person to have to cope with enabling him or her to transfer under cover from the car to the wheelchair and then set off to the building, preferably by means of a covered way. Where there is no direct link between parking and the building, then any building to be used by disabled persons—which means virtually

all buildings—should be provided with an adequate canopy over the front entrance so that persons waiting either to be admitted or for assistance, or persons dealing with keys and so forth, would be properly protected from the weather. At the front door, entry phones, bells and other means of calling for assistance should be mounted at a height that can easily be operated by persons in wheelchairs, in addition to those who are completely mobile. Wherever possible, disabled persons should be able to enter the building unaided. Calling for assistance is only really a rather poor substitute for the independence the disabled person would prefer to be able to exercise. Considerably more space is always taken up by ramp access as opposed to stairs. Ramps need to be surfaced with a non-slip finish, provided with hand rails and kerbs. They need to have landings and wherever possible should be under cover to prevent problems of frost and rain. In many cases, ramps need to be coupled with steps so that, especially for public buildings, people who are not wheelchair-bound are able to gain access via the steps, which—for most people—are easier to cope with than ramps. Especially, as mentioned before, this is the case for semi-ambulant persons.

2 Access within buildings needs to be well lit, floors should be covered with non-slip materials and all door openings should be without threshholds. For the semi-ambulant, grab rails should be provided. Where more than one disabled person is expected to use a particular building, adequate space needs to be provided for wheelchairs and/or semi-ambulant persons using walking aids to be able to pass in corridors. Light switches, power points and other controls must be mounted at an accessible height.

3 Toilet and wash facilities. As has already been mentioned additional space is required in these. Doors should either slide or open outwards in order to avoid the problem of someone falling down behind the doors. Some form of attracting attention or calling for assistance should be provided, usually by means of a cord hanging from the ceiling and connected to the caretaker's or warden's accommodation. Grab rails are needed to aid the person transferring from wheelchair to the toilet or bath and space should be provided for an assistant within the space. The WC pan should be mounted at such height that transfer is available without any change in level between wheelchair and WC pan. Whilst the wash hand basin should be able to be reached whilst sitting on the WC to enable the disabled person to wash his or her hands before having to transfer back onto the wheelchair, thus avoiding fouling the arms of the chair. In addition to this, the wash hand basin

should be at such a level that it can be conveniently used from the WC pan, or the wheelchair where a person goes into the toilet simply to wash his or her hands. To this end, it is necessary that the basin is clear underneath so that the chair can tuck underneath the basin. Taps need to be of the lever-arm variety for ease of operation not only by wheelchair-bound persons but also by people with arthritic hands or other problems that prevent the easy use of the hand. Location of facilities such as toilet paper holders, towels, etc. need to be very carefully considered. In bathrooms special hoists may be required to enable ease of transfer from wheelchair to bath. Special baths are also now available that allow the disabled person to enter the bath sideways or front on, and to take a bath in a sitting position. Showers are sometimes better than baths and in some cases it is possible to take the wheelchair into the shower. Thus special consideration needs to be taken into account for drainage.

4 Kitchens for disabled persons really need to be specifically designed for the individual case. However, some general points can be taken into account such as trying to avoid having doors between the kitchen and the living room. In addition to this, doors to cupboards should, wherever possible be eliminated or at least made to slide. Benches need to be lower so that they can be used from the wheelchair and need to be open underneath to allow the wheelchair to tuck under the bench while the person is working at that bench. This also applies to the kitchen sink, and taps should again preferably be of the lever-arm type. Power points, switches and controls all need to be mounted at a height that the disabled person can easily use, and all spaces where it is proposed to store things need to be within the fairly strict limitations that can be reached from the wheelchair; in other words they should be much higher off the floor and much lower in height at the top of the storage than would normally be the case. The openability of windows is discussed later.

5 Considerations for blind and deaf persons. When it comes to designing for blind persons, not only must the totally blind be considered but also the partially sighted. Here, high levels of illumination are necessary and very clear demarkation is required to avoid confusion whilst simple layouts and easy traffic routes through buildings should be provided. For blind persons, it is possible to change the texture of the floor covering at specific points to draw attention to the fact that changes are likely to occur, such as the approach to steps or the space outside a door, or any other dangerous situation. Other tactile guides that can be

provided are studs in a handrail indicating that one is coming to the top or bottom of a flight of stairs, or an intermediate landing. The number of studs can indicate the floor level, if necessary using three studs for the third floor, four studs for the fourth floor and so on. Room numbers and names can be of raised lettering or supplemented by signs in braille, whilst even noise and perfume can be used in a way which would aid blind, or semi-blind persons around a building. It is important that where there will be blind people using a building that no loose pieces of furniture or equipment should be left around, and also that change does not take place within the building without the blind persons being completely aware of this. For deaf persons, visual signals need to be provided where oral signals, such as bells and alarms, would normally be used. Door bells can be organized to flash the room lights either on or off, depending upon whether they are in use or not at the time. Large clear signs need to be provided in public buildings. The level of lighting needs to be high for deaf persons, as they will not hear the approach of anything which heralds danger such as vehicles.

6 Means of escape in case of fire. This is a particular problem for designers of buildings that are going to contain disabled persons. Greater fire protection may be necessary because of the time that is likely to elapse before the building can be vacated. This is because people may move more slowly or escape may have to take place from upper floors by means of lifts which in the normal course of events are not used for escape purposes. Some disabled persons may have to be vacated from higher floors or even from lower floors of buildings on stretchers requiring expert assistance; these assistants may have to return into the building in order to take more people out. All of this points to a higher level of fire separation and fire resistance within buildings housing disabled persons. Blind persons will need assistance in being directed to fire escape routes, whilst for those who are hard of hearing, visual alarms will be necessary in the form of flashing lights, which will also need to be wired to an emergency wiring system. Where deaf people are sleeping, it is possible to have some form of vibrator under the pillow which may be more satisfactory than a flashing light by the side of the bed. These vibrators, under the pillow or mattress, can also be used as a simple alarm mechanism for deaf persons to wake up in the mornings.

7 Other items requiring attention. As has already been mentioned, disabled persons tend to move more slowly and are therefore generally much less active than younger, healthier persons.

They therefore feel the cold more, and thus it is essential that background heating in buildings that are going to be used by disabled persons for any length of time needs to be at a higher temperature than that which would normally be expected. It is also essential that a disabled person should be able to use all facilities in buildings and to be able to enjoy the same. The heights of windows need to be carefully considered; persons permanently confined to a wheelchair need lower sills in order to be able to see out, than do people who are able to stand up. However, any space that is going to be used for relaxation—such as living rooms —even for ambulant people and for active younger people, should have window sills at such a height that a view of the garden or the immediate surroundings is able to be achieved from a sitting position (see Chapter 4). In addition to this, disabled persons need to be able to operate the windows and therefore the latches and locks need to be at a height that the disabled persons can cope with from their wheelchair, not only in order to open the window, but also to close the window. This can be a particular problem where windows open outwards and it is necessary to reach out through the window in order to bring the window in to close them. Further complications can occur where the window is over a bench as is often found in the kitchen. Power points, light switches, fuse boards and other controls should be mounted at a height that can easily be reached by disabled persons.

Generally speaking, therefore, designers should provide for disabled persons in designs of public buildings and also in private buildings wherever possible to ensure that disabled persons can live a full life quite independent of assistance. Disabled persons should be able to make use of all buildings which younger and more active persons are able to use, without the embarrassment of having to call for assistance or being afraid that they cannot use the toilet whilst they are out, which can result in their becoming housebound. In Britain it is now mandatory for all new buildings, except single-family houses to be constructed so that disabled persons have access to the ground floor and to all floors of office and shop buildings.

Whilst it is not necessary for all houses to be designed to cope with disabled persons, some houses will have to be designed specifically for individual disabled people who may have specific requirements whilst others will need to have disabled persons taken carefully into account in the original design. Wherever possible consideration should be given to disabled people in house design in order that they may visit houses of their friends and not feel in any way embarrassed in so doing. It is unlikely, however, that all houses will be designed to give maximum accessibility for disabled persons. Younger people who have disabled relatives or friends will probably wish to have their houses capable of receiving them or at least making their visit more comfortable. This can be done simply by having easy access to the house for a disabled person and slightly wider doors on the ground floor. Wherever possible, a fairly spacious downstairs toilet should be provided which the disabled person can use whilst visiting. When a disabled person does visit a house that is really only capable of coping with active people, there will almost always be somebody who can offer a certain amount of assistance—such as where there may be one step or a rather awkward threshhold detail to overcome—and possibly also even able to offer assistance in the toilet. Nevertheless, wherever it is possible to enable the disabled person to carry out all these activities independently, this is going to be a far better solution.

References
Extensions to buildings

Catt, R. and Catt, S. *The Conversion, Improvement and Extension of Buildings* (*Estates Gazette*: London, 1981).

Rehabilitation and conservation

Benson, J., Evans, B., Colomb P. and Jones, G. *The Housing Rehabilitation Handbook* (Architectural Press: London, 1980).
Dobby, A. *Conservation and Planning* (Hutchinson: London, 1978).

Needs of disabled persons in buildings

British Standards Institute BS4467: 1969 *Anthropometric and Ergonomic Recommendations in Designing for the Elderly* (BSI: London, 1969).
British Standards Institute BS5619: 1978 *Code of Practice for the Convenience of Disabled People* (BSI: London, 1978).
British Standards Institute BS5810: 1979 *Code of Practice for Access for the Disabled to Buildings* (BSI: London, 1979).
Goldsmith, S. *Designing for the Disabled* (RIBA: London, 1976).

of private sector housing in countries like Britain, the 'spec' built houses being constructed in countries that have traditionally had a greater number of specifically designed one-off units such as Australia and America are growing at a very great rate. Bureaucratic decisions have been made especially in the public sector about housing often by housing managers, sometimes following very careful research as is particularly the case, in Britain, with regard to the Parker Morris report and the earlier Tudor Walters report. A more recent example of these bureaucratic housing decisions in Britain was the one to build high-rise flats, fairly extensively for the public sector. These have, unfortunately, proved to be less than ideal for public sector tenants whose choice of housing is extremely limited. Some blocks have become unlettable with the result that a number of blocks have been either sold off to the private sector for refurbishment or they have been demolished.

Nowadays we are starting to see more attempts being put forward to present a coherent theory of the interaction between people and buildings. There are basically three groups of people who are contributing towards this. First of all there is the designer who has grown aware that the built environment does not have a simple deterministic effect upon people. Designers, therefore, want more feedback from the users often through the work of behavioural and social scientists. Secondly, psychologists have become more aware of the potential effects and importance of the environment; perhaps this is due to the increasing variation found in the built environment. When the environment was relatively stable and consistent it was not likely to produce differences in human behaviour but in recent years when the environment has undergone quite drastic changes, people's behaviour has become affected and psychologists are beginning to see that this is often very closely related to these changes in the environment. Thirdly, the public are now much better informed and more articulate than they were in the past. They are possibly more aware of the physical environment and are beginning to demand more and more sophisticated explanations from the experts they allow to build it.

Now that we have this awareness at least we are on the ladder, and the next step is to see how the design team can benefit from this awareness. It is going to be necessary for psychologists to evolve methods that will enable them to anticipate the behaviour of people in relation to the environment and to draw knowledge from the people themselves. The design team must work much more closely with the client formulating the brief (see chapter 2) and it must also make much more extensive use of the body of knowledge developed as a result of the above research, especially during the analysis and synthesis stages of the design process. Furthermore it is necessary for the client to be educated to appreciate the increasing role that the design team play in fashioning the environment and improving it so that various people who make use of the resultant spaces can work, play, live, worship, and study in them in a way which contributes to a better quality of life.

A criticism that has been levelled many times at the design team is that it has had, in the past, a rather dictatorial attitude towards its clients especially when it is designing for what is, in effect, a third person such as a local authority tenant, an employee or someone similar. Because of the role of the design team in the decision-making process it is probably inevitable that a certain dictatorial attitude will come forth. The leader of the design team is the architect, and architects are not famed for being committee members who are prepared to administer the wills of the committee. They are always conscious of the proverb that the camel was a horse designed by a committee, and many of the worst buildings that have been built in recent years—and no doubt those in the past as well—are those that were produced by committees rather than by a single, dedicated mind. However, that having been said we must accept that many buildings have been designed in a rather dictatorial manner and we have ended up with a type of architecture that has been sometimes referred to as the 'that's it' architecture.

User's concerns

There is obviously much need for better communication between the user and the designer. This tends to happen with most mass-produced goods (for example, motor cars where the vehicle simply would not sell unless it was designed in a way that was going to appeal to the customer). In recent years motor manufacturers have had to respond to the needs and concerns of purchasers, particularly with regard to improving fuel consumption and longevity. Buildings are, unfortunately, not always designed with quite such close collaboration in mind.

The design team must realize that their role is much more than simply building a building according to a certain brief; it must endeavour to understand the user's worries and concerns. For example, in many local authority flats private balconies have been provided to enable tenants to sit outside during good weather, and perhaps, to grow a few plants. In many cases these balconies have been used for drying washing. The design team's attitude may well be that the user should change his method of drying clothes and thus avoid destroying the amenity of the block of hanging clothes out on the balcony.

Conversely the design team should try to understand the client or the user's conflicts and worries. In this case there is the conflict between drying the clothes outside on the balcony and drying them internally by means of a tumbler dryer which perhaps the user can ill afford, either to purchase or to run. There is the worry that if he were to hang clothes out in an open drying space, say at the base of the block of flats, then the clothes that he could ill afford to replace would be stolen. Thus the amenity value at the balcony is sacrificed for the functional.

User's perception

Most people have a good idea about the type of house in which they would like to live. This often starts as early as childhood and when a British child is invited to draw a house, he or she invariably draws a detached building with a pitched roof, a fairly prominent front door, two or more windows and a chimney with curling smoke (see Figure 56). The actual picture that has been drawn is often much more related to the type of house that a child sees in a picture book, rather than the type of house in which he or she actually lives, or in which any of the people he or she visits lives.

Many of the children from high-rise blocks of flats have been known to draw their house in exactly this way whereas children in Northern Australia, for example, where there is a tradition for building houses on stilts, tend to draw little English cottages then push them up on stilts, showing a combination of awareness of environment with the typical stereotype picture-book house.

As people grow older and start to think a little bit more about their house, again the demand tends to be for a detached house, with a fairly traditional appearance. This is generally seen as the ideal and in Britain the little thatched country cottage has always featured very much in people's dreams. In Bruce Allsop's book *Towards a Humane Architecture* he quotes Marc-Antoine Laugier, who published his essay *Essai sur l'architecture* in 1752 when he identified the little hut as the essential form of classical architecture. This little hut had a pitched roof and columns, and in this essay we see three basic ideas of architecture propounded. First the 'little hut' being the basic home of man or God, the house, the shrine, the temple. Secondly, the monument based on the yoke and column usually with a flat top surface or roof and thirdly the device or tensile structure, which because of it

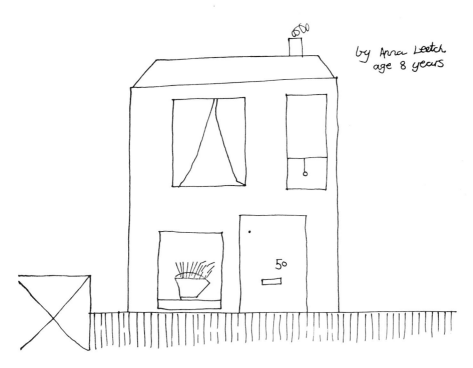

by Anna Leetch
age 8 years

Figure 56   Child's drawing of a house. Drawing courtesy of Anna Leetch, aged 8 years.

always having to be held lacks any powerful symbolism and is associated with temporal structures such as tents.

Although it is now possible to build waterpoof flat roofs the pitched roof remains, through this 'little hut' concept associated very much with shelter and the home. Whilst pitched or flat roofs and their associated overhang vary from country to country depending upon the climatic conditions a flat roof will only have the structure increased to cope with additional weight of snow and thus any national or regional form of architecture which truly reflects the climatic conditions, and the materials available is immediately lost. The symbolism of pitched roofs to houses manifests itself in many ways. At least three major building societies in Britain use derivations of the pitched roof in their 'logo' indicating the symbolic concept of protection. Flat-roof buildings, on the other hand, can easily be associated with the concept of the monument whilst monumental architecture tends to be associated with the grandiose and is thus not seen as being suitable for the dwelling place.

Another important element in the way a person sees his house, is reflected in the fact that detached houses tend to be favoured, in other words the householder likes to see it as a separate entity that can be clearly defined and marked out from its neighbours. People are rarely satisfied with a part of another building. This is especially the case when we come to large blocks of flats where the householder cannot really identify with the fact that his or her unit of living, their own 'little hut', is a box indicated externally only by the seventh and eighth windows along on the fifth level up. Apart from the fact that there is no way a person can really stamp their identity on the exterior of such a building, there is no way either that they can be seen identifying totally with this space that has been allocated to them.

Over the last few years in Britain, Australia and America there has been a move towards providing smaller more traditional one-, two- and three-storey houses. These are being built in smaller groups, perhaps placed around courtyards or small garden areas often incorporating the traditional terraced form of housing (see Figure 10). These have become especially popular in inner urban areas whilst in places where a little more land is available there has been a much greater move towards the detached house and the detached bungalow. It could be argued that the terraced house does not really give this clear identification of one's unit in the way that the detached house does, and this is certainly the case; however in urban areas and for smaller houses people often realise the advantages of terraced housing, or at least accept it, as being inevitable. Terraced housing is by no means as impersonal as a block of flats as it is still fairly easy to identify that part of the terrace that is yours and by careful design it is even possible to make this more noticeable. The staggering of houses is one way of providing this individuality, whilst in London the clear demarkation that results from the traditional extensions of party walls above the roof is a way of defining one's territory. In addition to this fences, and methods of marking the boundaries of gardens, lend themselves to individuality (see Figure 57). The design team should appreciate that people do want to mark their homes individually to show that it is their house. Unfortunately many fine terraces have been destroyed by this individuality. A good design should lend itself to the occupier's being able to stamp his individuality upon the house without destroying the unity of the terrace as a whole.

Nowadays where housing developments in both the public and private sectors tend to contain a large number of units special consideration needs to be made with regard to maintaining some

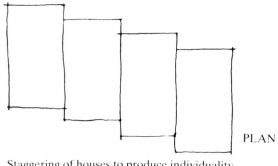

PLAN

Staggering of houses to produce individuality

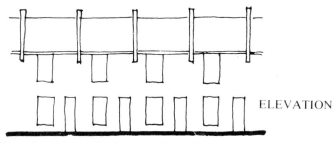

ELEVATION

Extending party walls above roofs produces individuality

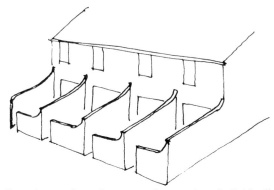

Boundary walls and gates used to produce individuality

Figure 57   Methods of showing individuality in a terrace.

form of individuality and smallness within particular schemes. People tend to identify with a small area in which they live—in fact, Nicholas Taylor calls this the urban village. It is important that the design of buildings within the urban village should be such that people can identify with their areas and also that the area can be sub-divided into small enough groups so that the hamlet, as it were, in which they live is able to be closely identified. Figure 10 shows a development of some thirty-two houses slotted into an existing urban fabric, because of the clear demarkation lines between these groups of houses and outside a very great sense of the urban village has been created within the area and everyone knows everyone else but not to the extent of interference whilst a very strong sense of belonging and community spirit exists, and this, in an inner London suburb where one would not necessarily expect to find such a closely knit group of people.

It is important that the balance between anonymity and isolation can be maintained in housing developments. Most people like to maintain a high degree of independence in their housing and to a very large extent want to keep themselves to themselves but they do not want to feel isolated. They want to be able to see their neighbours pass; they want to be aware of what is going on in their immediate environment and this of course only becomes possible when people are living on the ground, and with their eyes on the street. The concept of eyes on the street has already been discussed in Chapter 6, and the advantage of this from a security point of view, pointed out.

The reaction

Having accepted that the design team has a role to play in shaping the environment in which people are going to live, work, and play, and that it needs to understand the worries and concerns of the people who will use the buildings, and the spaces about these buildings, it is pertinent to look at how people do react towards their buildings. Obviously the best way for people to react is that of affection or even love.

The reaction of people to buildings is much the same as that from person to person where it is usually accepted that there are two principal ways in which love can develop. There is the love-at-first-sight and there is the love that grows on you. In some cases people are fortunate enough to be able to choose the buildings that they are going to have around them and in which they are going to live in the way they can choose their friends. But most people have their buildings thrust upon them, like their relatives, so how does the love develop in these cases?

If the buildings have all the necessary and desirable aesthetic and functional qualities, and are in a pleasant environment, like some of your relatives, you will grow to love them. If not, perhaps familiarity will eventually breed some form of respect and affection for the building, whilst in some cases indifference or even hostility will remain. These reactions, love, respect, indifference, and hostility, result in different methods of expression with regard to buildings.

Generally speaking, people who *love* their buildings will look after them. Some will, in fact, extend this to the extreme and smother their buildings with ornamentation such as carriage lamps, garden gnomes and many other external elements which too often reflect more money than taste.

The healthy *respect* for a building will also ensure that it is well looked after, and in the case of its being threatened, there will be people who will be prepared to take up its case to ensure that the best solution possible arises from many future proposals.

Indifference usually means that a building or space is ignored. In fact, there are certain people who are able to go through life with a total lack of environmental sensitivity; they can live totally oblivious to their surroundings and can only concern themselves with the things that actually belong to them. They can spend hours cleaning their car and then empty the ashtrays onto the ground immediately outside.

Hostility is usually reflected in outright damage to buildings in the form of vandalism, which usually involves wanton destruction of property which is invariably publicly owned. Whilst there is a certain amount of vandalism related to privately owned property, for the most part it is publicly owned property that is attacked. This is because public property is seen as 'theirs' and it is the 'them' against 'us' theory which means that 'their' property tends to be the victim of unwarranted attack. The stereotype vandal is invariably seen as the working-class youth, but of course we must never forget there are other vandals in society, the motor car, officialdom, tourism, planners, developers, and litterbugs.

Vandalism has been defined as falling into five categories: acquisitive, tactical, vindictive, play, and malicious. Acquisitive vandalism is really a form of theft, whereas tactical, vindictive, play, and malicious, are usually related to some form of pressure which is being seen to be applied to the perpetrators of the act of vandalism. Vandalism caused by play, such as footballs being kicked through windows, can sometimes be dismissed as accidental. However, generally speaking, property that is vandalized is usually already fairly badly kept, empty or not yet finished. In local authority housing vandalism tends to be greater in flatted estates than on estates of individual houses, and it tends to be worse on larger estates than on smaller estates.

In schools vandalism tends to be worse in areas of low socio-economic catchment, which invariably involve a fairly high mobility rate of staff and pupils that can have as much, if not more, bearing on the matter as the socio-economic situation of persons.

One of the most noticeable forms of vandalism is in the form of graffiti. It is rather interesting that very few people have ever seen graffiti being applied to a building, and when they do read graffiti they tend not to think of the person who wrote it as being a vandal, but as being perhaps a racist, a sexual deviant or mentally disturbed depending upon the message that has been inscribed. Graffiti is not new. There was graffiti in times of ancient Rome and certain graffiti is fairly well established and is almost institutionalized (for example, the desks in many public schools and the exterior and interior of New York Subway trains). In some circles graffiti has even been described as a twentieth-century art form. Also there is a certain amount of ideology with some of the messages that are applied, such as 'property is theft', or indeed messages being daubed on to embassy buildings where the protestors do not agree with the political beliefs of the party in power in the country represented by that particular embassy.

How can the designer combat vandalism? First of all it is essential to ensure that there is an absolute minimum amount of space on a design that is not actually allocated to some particular person or body who is responsible for its upkeep. Studies in the USA by Oscar Newman have shown that the allocation of front gardens to properties that previously opened straight out onto common space, not only resulted in a great reduction in vandalism but it also kept away people who were just passing by from the doors and windows of the individual houses, thus producing defensible space and greater security (see Chapter 6).

Certain amenities will always have to be under the control of the public authorities and here, where it is not possible to employ caretakers, it may be necessary to introduce some form of surveillance by electronic means. The design team role will also include ensuring that all components are sturdy and that materials chosen are not able to be broken or damaged easily. The use of toughened glass in bus shelters and telephone booths is a prime example of this. Bus shelters and telephone booths tend to suffer extensively from vandalism. This is partly due to the fact that these are places where people have to waste time waiting (like lift lobbies on high-rise blocks of flats) and when people are waiting there is a greater tendency for them to inflict damage on their surroundings. Once a vandal finds that the design and object defeats his vandalistic tendency then he is not likely to attempt to destroy a similar object in the future. In addition to this it is essential that any mess that he creates is very quickly cleared up, and the work repaired, perhaps two, three, four or even more times, eventually he will concede defeat. This has been found to be true in certain local authority areas with regard to the planting of trees; here trees that were vandalized and uprooted on successive evenings, have been replaced the following morning, and eventually the vandal has been defeated.

Obviously the choice of materials that are not going to withstand normal wear and tear and thus look shabby quickly will be ripe for the attention of a vandal. Cheap finishing materials, materials with exposed heads of screws (which invite people to undo the screws and start their own demolition), and small holes (where fingers can be pushed) all need to be designed out of particular objects. A simple picket fence near where the author lives was frequently vandalized, apparently by passing school children. The fence was constructed in the normal two-rail system with the pickets nailed to the rail top and bottom. It was a relatively simple matter for a child to put his foot against the bottom of the picket below the lowest rail, his hands at the top of the picket and pull, thus removing the picket from the rails. A simple solution to this was to provide metal bands continuously along the fence over the picket and therefore provide a more homogenous finish. It was then impossible to pull any one pailing off, without pulling vast numbers of pailings off, a task that would take far too long for the average school child on his way to or from school even to contemplate. A cheap and simple design solution prevented considerable anguish, untidyness and nuisance value, to say nothing of the cost of constant repair to the fence.

Conclusion

In order that fine architecture (rather than mere buildings) is produced, the design team must avail itself of the body of knowledge being developed by architectural psychologists. For the user and passer-by to experience true delight in relation to a building he must love, or, at least, respect it and thus his fears, concerns, likes and dislikes must be taken into account at the design stage. In other words the design team must 'let the people belong'.

References

Broady, M. 'Social theory of architectural design', *Arcaa*, January 1966, pp. 149–154.
Canter, D. and Lee, T. (eds) *Psychology and the Built Environment* (Architectural Press: London, 1974).
The Design Council *Designing Against Vandalism* (Heinemann: London, 1979).
Judd, B. and Dean J. L. (eds) *Medium Density Housing in Australia* (RAIA: London, 1983).
Taylor, N. *The Village in the City* (Temple Smith and *New Society*, 1973).
Ward, C. (ed.) *Vandalism* (Architectural Press: London, 1973).

10

Conclusion

The design solution for any building should be the result of the logical development of the brief. It should reflect fully the constraints and challenges of the climate of the locality in which the building stands together with those imposed by the site and the materials and technology which are available economically. The design will have to comply with all applicable current legislation and it will have to work in such a way that it answers the needs of the brief. Last, but by no means least, it must be aesthetically pleasing.

It is rarely possible to satisfy all these conflicting factors and usually compromises will have to be made. It is in the correct assessment of the priorities of these compromises that the design team will face its greatest challenge.

To be a work of architecture, rather than a mere building, the design will need a little more—an element of delight—a touch of a master's hand.

Index